I0890282

McMaster Journal of Theology and Ministry
ISSN 1481-0794
ISBN 978-1-60899-203-4

Editor
Wendy J. Porter
McMaster Divinity College

Managing Editor
Lois K. Dow
McMaster Divinity College
1280 Main Street West
Hamilton, Ontario, Canada L8S 4K1
email: mjtm@mcmaster.ca

McMaster Journal of Theology and Ministry is an electronic and print journal of McMaster Divinity College, in Hamilton, Ontario, Canada. It seeks to provide pastors, educators, and interested lay persons with the fruits of theological, biblical, and professional studies in an accessible form. It succeeds the Divinity College's former periodicals, the *Theological Bulletin*, *Theodolite*, and the *McMaster Journal of Theology*. Each volume covers an academic year (September to August). Reviews and articles are posted on the MacDiv website at:

http://www.mcmaster.ca/mjtm/

and beginning with Volume Nine (2007–2008), each volume is available around the end of September in hard copy as well.

McMaster Journal of Theology and Ministry is available on EBSCO Publishing's databases.

Manuscripts, books for review, and communications should be addressed to the Managing Editor through the email address on the journal website. Contributors are encouraged to use the style outlined in the Author Guide of Wipf and Stock, available at: http://wipfandstock.com.

All articles and book reviews are peer-reviewed for appropriate academic and professional standards.

Copies of the printed version can be ordered from Wipf and Stock Publishers in Eugene Oregon, USA, 97401, through their website, wipfandstock.com. Copies are also available at McMaster Divinity College.

For more information about McMaster Divinity College, please visit the College's website at www.macdiv.ca.

[*MJTM* 10 (2008–2009) 3–21]

Who Is the "Woman" in 1 Timothy 2?

John R. Master
Philadelphia Biblical University, Langhorne, PA
and
Jonathan L. Master
Capital Bible Seminary, Lanham, MD

Introduction

No passage of Scripture has engendered more debate regarding women in ministry than 1 Timothy 2. Although it does not speak directly to the question of female ordination, it has often been used in that regard. But it seems that some basic questions may not have received the attention they deserve.

Framework for This Discussion

Thomas Schreiner, in a book edited with Andreas Köstenberger, explores two of the options regarding 1 Timothy 2 and the implications of some of these options:

> What is meant by the word γυναῖκας in verse 9 and throughout the rest of this passage? Does it refer to women in general, or more specifically to wives? If it refers to wives both here and in subsequent verses, then women are not forbidden from teaching publicly in church. They are merely prohibited from teaching and exercising authority over their husbands.[1]

Elsewhere, various other questions have been asked about this text. The nature of "exercising authority" has been argued at length and, in our opinion, convincingly, in the volume edited by

1. Schreiner, "Interpretation of 1 Timothy 2:9–15," 92–93. Note that γυνή, γυναῖκες, γυναῖκα, and γυναῖκας used in this article are all case forms of the same Greek word.

Porter and Carson.[2] Another of the major disagreements relates to the question of the normative nature of 1 Timothy 2.[3] Some, such as Stendahl, would argue that Gal 3:28 needs to be understood as the determinative text, with 1 Timothy 2 and others reflecting the incorrect biases of the apostle Paul.[4] In this regard, it is also useful to note the categories into which Hoch divides his selected bibliography on the subject: non-evangelical egalitarian, evangelical egalitarian, and hierarchicalist. [5] Much of the literature seems to take this either/or stance.[6] Picking up on this general trend, Allison has pointed out the influence of one's presuppositional framework in dealing with the total biblical teaching on this subject. He writes,

> Among biblical scholars themselves, these issues above all others have pitted conservative against liberal, contributing to the downfall of the myth of value-free hermeneutics. The flood of obviously apologetic articles ("advocacy exegesis") claiming Paul for liberal or conservative views, either defending him against chauvinism or justifying his subordination of women, has sharpened our awareness of the problem of the Pauline "canon within the canon," but is also politicizing the exegetical enterprise in general when it involves these issues.[7]

For the record, our conclusion on this matter is that 1 Timothy 2 ought to be considered normative. We reject (and hope to avoid) the pitfall of creating a canon within the canon. We are also persuaded that the teaching of 1 Timothy 2 is not merely a parochial matter related to the particularities of the Ephesian church in particular, nor was it normative simply for the ancient church. We are persuaded that the teaching of this

2. Köstenberger, "Syntactical Background Studies to 1 Tim 2.12."

3. For one of many examples of this, see the point and counterpoint articles of Fee, "Issues in Evangelical Hermeneutics, Part III," and Waltke, "1 Timothy 2:8–15: Unique or Normative? A Response to Gordon Fee."

4. Stendahl, *Bible and the Role of Women*.

5. Hoch, "The Role of Women in the Church."

6. Cf. Wall, "Wifely Submission," 272, and Allison, "Let Women Be Silent," 27.

7. Allison, "Let Women Be Silent," 27.

text, such as it is, should be considered as both applicable and authoritative for all churches.

But it is to Schreiner's original question that we turn. Who are the "women" about whom Paul writes?

The English Translation Options

Underlying much of the discussion regarding the male/female relationship appears to be a semantic confusion based on the lack of one-for-one correspondence between the English words for wife/woman/female and husband/man/male with the Greek and Hebrew terms used to express these ideas. Such differences may serve to obscure our understanding of the meaning of the original text. English translations use three sets of words "male/female," "man/woman," and "husband/wife." Greek and Hebrew, on the other hand, basically use only two sets of terms to cover these same English concepts: one for "male/female," marking clear sexual differentiation, and another that can be translated either "man/woman" or "husband/wife."

Though most mainstream translations render the word γυνή (*gunē*) as "woman" in 1 Timothy 2,[8] it is by no means certain that γυνή should be translated in this way. The King James Version, which has exercised a massive (and justly deserved) influence over subsequent English translations, renders γυνή as "wife" 84 times and "woman" 102 times. The KJV consistently renders the term "woman" 16 times in 1 Corinthians 11 and twice in 1 Timothy 2. However, more recently, some translations—such as the ESV, which renders γυνή "woman" in 1 Timothy 2—render the same term differently in 1 Cor 11:3 where headship and submission are equally in view. There are probably several reasons for this, but it is not an inconsequential choice, given the options in English. Here, for instance, are the five definitions of "woman" given by the *Merriam-Webster's Collegiate Dictionary*, eleventh edition:

1 a : an adult female person

8. NASB, NKJV, ESV, NET, TNIV, HCSB, and NIV.

b : a woman belonging to a particular category (as by birth, residence, membership, or occupation)—usu. used in combination e.g. councilwoman
2 : womankind
3 : distinctively feminine nature: womanliness
4 : a woman who is a servant or personal attendant
5 a chiefly dial : wife
b : mistress
c : girlfriend

Note that at least the first four of these definitions could essentially be used interchangeably with the English word "female." In fact, the primary definition of "woman" in English is "an adult female person." This presents a problem when deciding how to translate various biblical passages, because, in both the Old and New Testaments, the linguistic options are decidedly different.

The Burden of Proof

The difficulty is that the term "woman," as it is used in English, is a term denoting gender primarily. On the other hand, the term "wife," while also being gender-specific, denotes a particular role and a particular stage of life. The question is, when we come to 1 Timothy 2, which should be our default translation? Should we assume that Paul is making a point about gender roles, or should we assume that he is talking about roles within the family?

Although we must be cautious in making sweeping claims, no doubt some of the confusion results from the cultural differences between our society and that of the New Testament. It does seem as if the category of adult, never-married women was far less widespread than it is today. Hommes writes, "The Graeco-Roman world of Paul's day hardly knew the concept of an unmarried woman. A girl married early (age 14–17)."[9] The terms translated "man" and "woman" did not simply, or even

9. Hommes, "Let Women Be Silent in Church," 14, n. 11.

mostly, mean "male" and "female" in terms of simple gender distinction—certainly not in Paul's writings. House correctly writes, "emphatic sexual differentiation is mostly expressed in biblical Greek by ἄρσεν and θῆλυ."[10]

However, the word γυνή is a relatively popular one. It is used in the LXX in 1139 verses, for a total of 1289 times and in the New Testament 215 times in 194 verses.[11] We have briefly examined each of these, and find that they fit our hypothesis as far as we can see (obviously we looked more closely at the New Testament uses); but in an article of this size, we must consolidate our research parameters. Therefore, we begin by examining the LXX of Genesis (to which Paul alludes in 1 Timothy 2), Philo, the Pastoral Epistles, and one other important passage parallel to 1 Timothy 2. By examining each of these, we can see which of the two English translations—"wife" or "woman"—would be the expected one, all other things being equal, and, in turn, which translation needs to meet the higher burden of contextual proof.

The LXX of Genesis and Philo

Since Paul cites Genesis as part of the explanation for his injunction in 1 Timothy 2, we must begin by examining the usage of γυνή in Genesis. In addition, we will briefly look at some particularly relevant examples in Philo for comparison.

Use in Genesis. Both the Old and New Testaments use particular words that refer to sexual differentiation, and more general words that are translated either "woman" or "wife," (or "man" or "husband"). The earliest usage of these distinctive words is in Gen 1:27 ("male and female created he them," using זכר (*zākār*), LXX ἄρσεν (*arsen*) and נקבה [*n^e^qebah*], LXX θῆλυ [*thēlu*]). Next, in Gen 2:22, אשה [*ishshah*] (LXX γυναῖκα) is first used, speaking of the woman/wife. Genesis 1 implies nothing other than the sexual distinction. In Genesis 2, however, the marriage relationship is in view, and different words are used

10. House, "Speaking of Women," 310.

11. This is according to a search on *BibleWorks* software.

(cf. esp. Gen 2:24, אִישׁ [*îsh*], LXX ἄνθρωπος [*anthrōpos*] and אִשָּׁה, LXX γυναῖκα). Note that in Genesis, the term אִשָּׁה is always translated by γυνή in the LXX and has the idea of "wife." In every use of γυνή in Genesis (151 times), it is always used in a marriage context referring to a "wife," (though it is possible to read Gen 14:16 as an exception).[12]

Along the same lines, the term נְקֵבָה is always used in Genesis with an emphasis on sexual differentiation. It is used in Gen 1:27 and in 5:2 (which is a reference back to Gen 1:27). The three other uses of the term (Gen 6:19; 7:3, 9) refer to the animals taken into the ark. "Marriage" is not part of the context of the word usage in Genesis. And in each case the LXX translates with the term θῆλυ. The LXX also uses θῆλυ another time in Gen 7:16 where it is employed to differentiate the sexes of the animals entering the ark. Neither the Hebrew נְקֵבָה nor Greek θῆλυ appear ever to be used in a specific marriage context in Genesis.[13]

The term זָכָר, translated "male" in Gen 1:27, is found 14 times in Genesis. It is not only used in the texts mentioned above regarding ἄρσεν and θῆλυ, but is found in Genesis 17 four times where it is used in the context of "male" circumcision. It appears an additional four times for the "male" circumcision of the Shechemites in Genesis 34. Throughout the Old Testament זָכָר is used to specifically identify gender without reference to marital status and is used to refer even to animals for sacrifice. In the LXX of Genesis it is always translated ἄρσεν.[14]

12. NASB (emphasis added): "He brought back all the goods, and also brought back his relative Lot, with his possessions, and also the *women*, and the people."

13. The term only appears eight times in Genesis.

14. In Lev 20:13 the term is also used to indicate that illicit sexual behavior is in view. The term אִישׁ is used along with זָכָר. This suggests what is forbidden may specifically, in this verse, be a married man having sexual relationships with a "male."

In the whole LXX, the term ἄρσεν (translated "male") is used consistently to refer to the male gender, predominantly as a translation of the Hebrew root זכר.[15]

Use in Philo. This same pattern holds true in Philo. θῆλυ occurs 74 times. We have examined each use, paying special attention to those times when θῆλυ is used in close proximity with γυνή. Our intent was to see how the gender-specific terms were used, compared with those that can also denote marital status. The following quotation is illustrative.

> But such great anxiety and energy is displayed by the law in attaining the object of training and exercising the soul so as to fill it with courage, that it has even descended to particulars in the matter of raiment, enjoining what men ought to wear, and prohibiting with all its might a *man* [ἀνήρ] from wearing the garments of a *woman* [γυνή], in order that no trace of shadow of the *female* [θῆλυς] may be attached to the *male* [ἄρσην] part of mankind, to its discredit; for the law, being at all times in perfect consistency according with nature, desires to establish laws which shall be akin to and in perfect harmony with one another from beginning to end, even in those minute points which, by reason of their insignificance, appear to be beneath the notice of ordinary legislators.[16]

Again note Philo's use of these terms.

> But we must begin our explanation of these mysteries in this way. A *husband* [ἀνήρ] unites with his *wife* [γυνή], and the *male human being* [ἄρσην] with the *female human being* [θῆλυς] in a union which tends to the generation of children, in strict accordance with and obedience to nature. But it is not lawful for virtues, which are the parents of many perfect things, to associate with a mortal husband. But they, without having received the power of generation from any other being, will never be able by themselves alone to conceive anything.[17]

15. McComiskey, "zākār," indicates that this Hebrew word "denotes the male of humans or animals." 243. Cf. Clements, "זָכָר zākhār," 82, 84–85.
16. Yonge, *Works of Philo*, 641 (emphasis mine).
17. Yonge, *Works of Philo*, 84 (emphasis mine).

This last text, in particular, shows Philo's usage of these critical terms. ἀνήρ (*anēr*) and γυνή are not the terms used to specify simple sexual distinction.

The New Testament Passages

In order to understand better which translation makes the best sense in the context of 1 Timothy 2, we must briefly examine the New Testament passages that use γυνή. This will provide us with some guidelines about which translation deserves to be the default setting when we come to 1 Timothy 2, and which one justifies the higher burden of contextual proof.

It should be noted at the outset that, in our examination of the New Testament texts, we were unable to find a use of γυνή that could not be understood as "wife." However, two sections deserve particular emphasis: the Pastoral Epistles, and 1 Corinthians 14, which is often assumed to be parallel in its teaching to 1 Timothy 2.

Pastoral Epistles. The term γυνή is used ten times in the Pastoral Epistles. Strikingly, the ESV, to use just one representative translation, always translates γυνή as "wife" in the pastorals, *except* in 1 Timothy 2.[18] In some cases, such as 1 Tim 3:2, 3:12, 5:9, and Tit 1:6, the term contextually must refer to a wife and not the more general idea conveyed by the term "woman." In fact, every occurrence of this term in the pastorals *could* be translated either "wife" or "wives."[19] That is to say, most of the instances of γυνή in the pastorals actually require the translation "wife"; and those that do not absolutely demand it from the immediate context contain nothing to prevent such a translation and much to commend it.

18. The texts are 1 Tim 2:9, 10, 11, 12, 14; 3:2, 11, 12; 5:9; Tit 1:6.

19. Interestingly, Tucker and Liefeld recognize these two translational possibilities in discussing deaconesses but do not discuss the same issue in Appendix B which specifically relates to exegetical issues (Tucker and Liefeld, *Daughters of the Church*, 86).

If we expand the parameters to include the entire Pauline corpus, we find a similar phenomenon.[20] The ESV, for example, translates approximately two-thirds of these as "wife" and not "woman." If we eliminate 1 Timothy 2, the percentage rises even higher. Also, in the ESV translation of 1 Corinthians 11, the translation moves back and forth between "wife" and "woman"; so even the translation "woman" in 1 Corinthians 11 is often used as a stylistic replacement for the "wives" in question.

Although it is beyond the scope of this paper to examine every Pauline passage, having looked at all of them, we can see none that demand being translated in strictly gender-oriented terms. In any case, it is inarguable—and on this the English translations are in agreement—that, at the very least, the entire Pauline use of γυνή is weighted far more toward the translation "wife" than "woman."

First Corinthians 14. First Corinthians 14 is the passage often viewed as the closest parallel to 1 Timothy 2 in terms of its teaching on women. This is the passage in which some argue that Paul is saying more or less the same thing to the Corinthian believers as he says to the Ephesians in 1 Timothy 2. In fact, these are the only passages that specifically prohibit "women" from teaching.[21] House writes:

> The teaching of Paul in 1 Timothy 2:8–15 seems to have more in common with 1 Corinthians 14:33b–35 than with 1 Corinthians 11:2–16. Whereas 1 Corinthians 11:2–16 recognizes the prophetic function of the woman under the control of the Spirit, 1 Timothy 2:8–15, along with 1 Corinthians 14:33b–35, prohibits vocal expression or position of leadership over men in the congregation. These two passages have similar emphases."[22]

But two questions immediately present themselves when examining these parallels. First, what is the λαλεῖν (*lalein*, to

20. Rom 7:2; 1 Cor 5:1; 7:1–6, 10–16, 27, 29, 33–34, 39; 9:5; 11:3, 5–15; 14:34–35; Gal 4:4; Eph 5:22–25, 28, 31, 33; Col 3:18–19; 1 Tim 2:9–15; 3:2, 11–12; 5:9; Tit 1:6.

21. Powers, *Ministry of Women*, 69.

22. Oepke, "ἀνήρ," 362.

speak) from which they were forbidden in 1 Corinthians 14? And second, more to the point, is there any indication in the text as to whether the translation should be rendered "women" or "wives"?

If λαλεῖν absolutely forbids all speaking, then this is hard to reconcile with Paul's assumption, in this very letter, that women will indeed speak within the public assembly (1 Cor 11:5).[23] In 1 Corinthians 11, it is assumed that they will pray and prophesy, and Paul's admonition is that they not do so with an uncovered head. In addition, if Paul had intended merely to prohibit women from preaching, might he not have used one of the more commonly-used words for teaching, preaching, or proclamation?[24] Further, it should be noted that Paul's overall concern in this passage is for orderliness. The discussion of "women" lies between v. 33 and v. 40, both of which emphasize orderliness and avoiding confusion. Of course, it is possible that Paul used λαλεῖν to denote preaching or formal teaching (but not prophesying or praying), and it is possible that this would be a natural and necessary application of the admonition to avoid confusion in the service, but all this seems unlikely.

More significantly, it is widely acknowledged (virtually all modern translations reflect this), that the women in question were indeed married, since the following verse enjoins them to save their questions for their husbands at home (v. 35).

In short, it seems unlikely that 1 Corinthians 14 is about preaching or teaching within the church service; but regardless, it is almost certainly not making a point related primarily to gender differentiation, but rather one in which γυνή is being employed in reference to married women.

23. Some have argued—though it seems difficult to defend—that this is a private, not corporate context, since v. 17 summarizes Paul's instruction and regards it as part of their "[coming] together" as a body. For an alternative view, see Holmyard, "Does 1 Corinthians 11:2–16 Refer to Women Praying and Prophesying in Church?"

24. On this, see the discussion in Powers, *Ministry of Women*, 61–62.

Burden of Proof Concluded

Based on the use of γυνή in the LXX of Genesis, the use in Philo's Koine, the Pastorals and broader Pauline usage, and the parallel passage in 1 Corinthians 14, translating γυνή in 1 Timothy 2 as "wife" instead of "woman" is quite possible. More than that, we would argue that to assume that the translation "wife" requires a higher burden of proof is to upend precisely where the real burden of proof lies. The other passages even suggest that "wife" is in fact the more likely translation.

1 Timothy 2:8–15: Observations and Questions

We are now at the point where we can look at 1 Timothy 2 directly. Several important questions need to be asked. First, why would the terms that explicitly point out sexual differentiation not be used? After all, Paul felt it worth the change to switch from using ἀνθρώπων (a masculine word that can mean a human being generally) in v. 5 to ἄνδρας (a man/husband) in v. 8. At first glance, this would appear to have some significance. At the very least, one might say that Paul was picking his specific words carefully. If he had wanted to use the term for "female," that was certainly an option available to him.[25]

In addition, many have pointed out that there are parallels between Paul's teaching about authority here in 1 Timothy 2 and his teaching in Ephesians 5.[26] It should be noted that this is essentially the rationale offered by Hugenberger (though he connects 1 Timothy 2 with 1 Peter 3) and rejected by Schreiner. To quote Schreiner at length:

> The idea that wives rather than women in general are the referent has been argued at some length by Gordon Hugenberger. He contends that a reference to women and men in general is not demanded in writing to the church, for Peter, in a text (1 Pet. 3:1–7) that is quite similar to 1 Timothy 2:9–15, only refers to husbands and wives . . . In

25. Regarding the expectations related to γυνή, "The Graeco-Roman world of Paul's day hardly knew the concept of an unmarried woman. A girl married early (age 14–17)" (Hommes, "Let Women Be Silent in Church," 14, n. 11).

26. Cf. Barrett, *Pastoral Epistles*, 55; Prohl, *Women in the Church*, 32–33.

addition, elsewhere in Paul the terms γυνή and ἀνήρ usually refer to wives and husbands, not to women and men in general. Further, he asserts that the parallels between Titus 2:4–5 and 1 Peter 3:1–7 are crucial for establishing the referent in 1 Timothy 2. In fact, Hugenberger thinks that the extensive verbal and conceptual parallels between 1 Timothy 2 and 1 Peter 3 "must be determinative for our exegesis" of 1 Timothy 2. He believes it is unthinkable that no discussion of the family would occur in 1 Timothy.

The burden of Hugenberger's argument is that parallel texts show that Paul refers to husbands and wives in 1 Timothy 2:8–15. He especially leans on the parallels between 1 Timothy 2:8–15 and 1 Peter 3:1–7, seeing the latter as "determinative" for the meaning of the former. However, the texts hardly correspond in every respect, despite some impressive parallels. For instance, the 1 Peter text refers to *nonbelieving* husbands (3:1). And in 3:7 husbands are addressed in terms of their specific responsibilities to their wives (cf. Eph. 5:25–30, 33; Col. 3:19). No admonition for husbands regarding their relationship with their wives is present in 1 Timothy 2. Finally, it is obvious that Peter has husbands and wives in view in 1 Peter 3 since he says wives should be subject to their *own* (ἰδίοις) husbands (v. 1; cf. v. 5). It is precisely this kind of clarifying evidence that 1 Timothy 2:8–15 lacks, with the result that most scholars detect a reference to men and women in general.

It is hardly impressive to say that elsewhere γυνή and ἀνήρ refer to husbands and wives since in those texts a reference to husbands and wives is indicated plainly in the context, and such passages are not even debated with respect to this issue. Some examples will illustrate how clear the evidence is: "the married woman" (ἡ ὕπανδρος γυνή, Rom. 7:2); "each man should have his own wife" (τὴν ἑαυτοῦ γυναῖκα, 1 Cor. 7:2); "to the married" (τοῖς γεγαμηκόσιν, 1 Cor. 7:10); "if any brother has a wife" (ἀδελφὸς γυναῖκα ἔχει, 1 Cor. 7:12); "her husband" (ὁ ἀνὴρ αὐτῆς, 1 Cor. 7:39); "Let them ask their own husbands at home" (τοὺς ἰδίους ἄνδρας 1 Cor. 14:35); "I betrothed you to one husband" (2 Cor. 11:2); "More are the children of the desolate one than of the one having a husband" (Gal. 4:27); "wives being subject to their own husbands" (αἱ γυναῖκες τοῖς ἰδίοις ἀνδράσιν, Eph. 5:22); "husband of one wife" (1 Tim. 3:2; cf. 1 Tim. 3:12; 5:9; Titus 1:6); "Instruct the young women to be lovers of their husbands (φιλάνδρους) . . . being subject to their own husbands" (τοῖς ἰδίοις ἀνδράσιν, Titus 2:5). By way of contrast,

> the lack of such qualifications in 1 Corinthians 11:2–16 shows that Paul is not referring to just husbands and wives, but to men and women in general. In Colossians 3:18–19, Paul could conceivably be referring to men and women in general, but the context (the next pericope deals with relations between parents and children, 3:20–21) and the call to "love your wives" (3:19) reveal that husbands and wives are in view. The very lack of such specificity in 1 Timothy 2:8–15 has rightly led most commentators to see a reference to men and women in general. Hugenberger demands that the Pauline usage elsewhere must obtain here, but he fails to notice the significant contextual differences between these other texts and 1 Timothy 2 and ends up imposing these other texts on the interpretation of 1 Timothy 2.[27]

Despite the frequent appeals to "most commentators" at key points in his argument, Schreiner does make some significant points. He acknowledges that much of the Pauline usage supports Hugenberger's conclusion. But essentially, he disagrees on two points. The first is the interpretation of 1 Corinthians 11. Without re-arguing the merits of our particular view, it is hard to argue, as Schreiner does, that 1 Corinthians 11 is a clear model that must then determine how we understand 1 Timothy 2. Second, he disagrees about the similarities between 1 Timothy 2 and other passages that do refer to husbands and wives using the same terminology as 1 Timothy 2. Although Schreiner essentially acknowledges that the majority (we would argue all) of the Pauline usages of γυνή are in concert with Hugenberger's understanding of γυνή in 1 Timothy 2, he nonetheless places the burden of proof on those who would argue that this use is like all the other Pauline usages. In fact, it would seem more reasonable to conclude, based on the biblical usage and the available Koine parallels, that the burden of proof lies in the other direction. Rather it seems that those who would translate and interpret this as referring to all females and all males have a higher burden of proof to meet in their interpretation.

27. Schreiner, "Interpretation of 1 Timothy 2:9–15," 92–93.

Contextual Arguments

We have argued, based on the LXX of Genesis, the text of Philo, and the major New Testament texts, that the burden of proof—at least initially—must be placed on those who would translate these as, effectively, "male" and "female." But burden of proof arguments can be tricky, and they are nearly always debatable. In fact, regardless of who bears the greater burden of proof, there are two significant contextual arguments that suggest that it is "wives" rather than "women" who are Paul's concern in this chapter.

First, it should be noted that Paul refers to the relationship of Adam and Eve (1 Tim 2:13) in order to support his conclusion. Many have argued, quite rightly, that this shows that Paul's comments are not just parochial; nor are they based merely on the particular situation of the church in Ephesus (whatever that might have been). But, in addition to the transcultural application of Paul's command demanded by his appeal to creation there is also another quite significant point to note. The particular allusion is to creation, but it is to the account in Genesis 2, not to Genesis 1.[28] Genesis 1 does not indicate that Adam was created before Eve but rather that God created them "male" and "female." The order of creation is found in Genesis 2 where the context relates to the marriage relationship. As previously noted, the term γυνή is first used in the LXX in Gen 2:22. The "male" and "female" terms are used in Genesis 1 and not in Genesis 2.[29] In other words, the terminology used by the author of 1 Tim 2:14 does not point to the creation account of Genesis 1 where the

28. We want to be very clear that we are not advocating that either Genesis 1 or Genesis 2 deserves priority. Both are in harmony and do not disagree with one another, though they do have different emphases.

29. Grenz and Kjesbo, *Women in the Church*, 163, note this: "In the Genesis 2 narrative he simply addresses her with the accolade *female*." Where the term נקבה is not used in Genesis 2, the term אשׁה is used, and, while translated "female" in some texts, it may be better understood as the "female in a paired relationship" (cf. Gen 7:2 and Exod 3:22).

term "female" is used but rather to Genesis 2, with its emphasis on the covenantal marriage relationship. First Timothy 2:14, following Genesis 2, does not use θῆλυ either, since that would communicate exclusively sexual differentiation from the man. Rather the reference is to a wife who has entered into the covenant of marriage with her husband.

It goes without saying that the headship of the husband over the wife is not an unusual note for Paul to strike; and it is notably struck by Peter also in one of the significant passages employed by Hugenberger (cf. Eph 5; Tit 2:5; 1 Pet 3:5–6).[30]

But there are other textual clues indicating that γυνή might better be translated "wife" and not "woman" in this passage. First, whatever the expression σωθήσεται δὲ (1 Tim 2:15a) means, it does result from the bearing of children (διὰ τῆς τεκνογονίας). On its face, it seems unusual that Paul would intend to elevate the behavior of an unwed mother as the high and noble calling to which Christian women were called. Yet virtually all commentators and translators consider that this expression has reference to the γυνή spoken of in the preceding context. In other words, vv. 13–15 is given as support for what has just been said in vv. 11–12. In that case, it would be inappropriate to think of the γυνή in vv. 11–12 as simply a "woman," if, by that, one intended to convey merely a person of the female gender. Unless she were actually a wife, the passage would seem to elevate sexual impropriety.

Finally, in addition to these arguments, there is the parallel with 1 Peter 3. The similarities between the admonitions in these chapters are remarkable.[31] Yet, on this, Schreiner is essentially correct: some of the clarifying factors present in 1 Peter 3 are not explicit in 1 Timothy 2. However, taken together with the linguistic evidence and context of 1 Timothy 2, Hugenberger (along

30. Prohl, *Women in the Church*, 35, cf. 37, writes, "As we now go on to the next chapter and a consideration of the Old Testament passages referred to in the restrictions, we shall note how the evidence piles up in support of our contention that the Christian wife is the woman involved; that there is no law of creation which makes women in general subordinate to men in general, but that there is a law of creation which makes the husband the head of the wife."

31. Hugenberger, "Women in Church Office."

with Powers and others) seems to have solid reasons for asserting the essential parallel with 1 Peter 3.

Conclusion

In short, the use of the term γυνή in the LXX and Philo, the general use of the term γυνή in the Pastoral Epistles, the marriage context of 1 Corinthians 14 (the other Pauline passage that is claimed to prohibit females from teaching), the Old Testament context of the citation in 1 Tim 2:14, and the positive reference to childbearing, suggest the term γυνή in 1 Tim 2:11–15 is better translated "wife."[32]

Had Paul wanted to say that no female could teach a male, he could have used the terms "male" and "female" that he used elsewhere (i.e., Rom 1:27; Gal 3:28). The terms that he did use are highly suggestive, and most appropriate for speaking of the husband and wife relationship, not simply the male/female sexual distinction. Headship and submission are significant Pauline themes when the subject is marriage, so this would not have been an unusual note for him to strike in this context. In short, 1 Timothy 2 does not prohibit females serving in authority over males provided that it is not a wife over her husband and provided there is not some other revelation—such as that concerning elders—that might prohibit it.[33] In this view, γυνή is understood in this text in precisely the same manner as it is understood in every other instance in the Pastoral Epistles.

Paul wrote 1 Timothy 2 to prevent Christian practice from undermining the structure of the Christian household. Paul gives binding commands for the proper boundaries of the γυναῖκες in the church. They were not to teach or exercise authority over

32. Barnett, "Wives and Women's Ministry."

33. The conclusions of this paper do not cover the question of the role of the woman in the church, an issue that deserves further study. For a recent discussion of this, see Barnett, "Wives and Women's Ministry." The church, with the equality of male and female, does not vitiate the headship/submission relationship established in the marriage covenant.

their husbands. To do so would violate the vital ordinance of marriage—rooted in creation—to which Paul gave so much attention elsewhere, and which stood as an enduring illustration of Christ and his church.

Bibliography

Allison, Robert W. "Let Women Be Silent in the Churches (1 Cor. 14:33b–36): What Did Paul Really Say, and What Did It Mean?" *JSNT* 32 (1988) 27–60

Barnett, Paul W. "Wives and Women's Ministry (1 Timothy 2:11–15)." *EvQ* 61 (1989) 225–38.

Barrett, C.K. *The Pastoral Epistles*. Oxford: Clarendon Press, 1963.

Clements, R. E. "זָכָר zākhār." In *TDOT* 4:82–87.

Fee, Gordon D. "Issues in Evangelical Hermeneutics, Part III: The Great Watershed—Intentionality and Particularity/Eternity: 1 Timothy 2:8–15 as a Test Case." *Crux* 26 (1990) 31–37.

Grenz, Stanley J. and Denise Muir Kjesbo. *Women in the Church: A Biblical Theology of Women in Ministry*. Downers Grove: InterVarsity Press, 1995.

Hoch, Carl B., Jr. "The Role of Women in the Church: A Survey of Current Approaches." *Grace Theological Journal* 82 (1987) 250–51.

Holmyard, Harold R. III. "Does 1 Corinthians 11:2–16 Refer to Women Praying and Prophesying in Church?" *BibSac* 154 (1997) 461–72.

Hommes, N. J. "Let Women Be Silent in Church." *CTJ* 4 (1969) 5–22.

House, H. Wayne. "The Speaking of Women and the Prohibition of the Law." *BibSac* 145 (1988) 301–17.

Hugenberger, Gordon P. "Women in Church Office: Hermeneutics or Exegesis? A Survey of Approaches to 1 Tim 2:8–15" *JETS* 35 (1992) 431–60.

Köstenberger, Andreas J. "Syntactical Background Studies to 1 Tim 2:12 in the New Testament and Extrabiblical Greek Literature." In *Discourse Analysis and Other Topics in Biblical Greek*, edited by Stanley E. Porter and D. A. Carson, 156–79. JSNTSup 113. Sheffield: Sheffield Academic Press, 1995.

McComiskey, Thomas Edward. "zākār."In *TWOT* 2:243.

Merriam-Webster's Collegiate Dictionary. 11th ed. Springfield, MA: Merriam-Webster, 2003.

Oepke, Albrecht. "ἀνήρ." In *TDNT* 1:360–63.

Powers, W. *The Ministry of Women in the Church: Which Way Forward?* Maricksville, Australia: SPCKA, 1996.

Prohl, Russell C. *Women in the Church*. Grand Rapids: Eerdmans, 1957.

Schreiner, Thomas R. "An Interpretation of 1 Timothy 2:9–15." In *Women in the Church: An Analysis and Application of 1 Timothy 2:9/15*, edited by Andreas J. Köstenberger and Thomas R. Schreiner, 85–120. 2nd ed. Grand Rapids: Baker Academic, 2005.

Stendahl, K. *The Bible and the Role of Women: A Case Study in Hermeneutics*. Philadelphia: Fortress Press, 1966.

Tucker, Ruth A. and Walter L. Liefeld. *Daughters of the Church.* Grand Rapids: Zondervan Academie Books, 1987.

Wall, Robert. "Wifely Submission in the Context of Ephesians." *CSR* 17 (1988) 272–85.

Waltke, Bruce K. "1 Timothy 2:8–15: Unique or Normative? A Response to Gordon Fee." *Crux* 28 (1992) 22–27.

Yonge, C. D. *The Works of Philo: Complete and Unabridged.* Peabody, MA: Hendrickson, 1993.

[*MJTM* 10 (2008–2009) 22–51]

PENAL SUBSTITUTION IN PERSPECTIVE: RE-EVALUATING THE ARTICULATION AND APPLICATION OF THE DOCTRINE

Patrick Franklin
McMaster Divinity College, Hamilton, ON

1. *Introduction*

> Bearing shame and scoffing rude, in my place condemned he stood—
> Sealed my pardon with his blood: Hallelujah, what a Savior!
> – Philip P. Bliss

It is no secret that, in recent times, the doctrine of penal substitution has fallen into disrepute. It is accused of being outdated and irrelevant to contemporary culture, degradingly anthropomorphic in its view of God, and morally reprehensible in its social implications. While there is a degree of truth to these charges, they fundamentally misunderstand and misrepresent the penal substitution view. What they attack is a crude caricature, not the genuine doctrine as articulated by its best proponents.

In contrast, penal substitution is a legitimate and relevant representation of the biblical doctrine of atonement. The problem with this metaphor is not primarily its *formulation* (although certain qualifications need to be made), but its *application*. In particular, problems arise when the penal substitution metaphor is viewed in isolation from other atonement metaphors, when it becomes a dominant or controlling metanarrative, or when it is converted mechanistically into a methodology for evangelism. Essentially, each of these errors leads to gospel reductionism. In order to develop the above points, the paper first examines the doctrine of penal substitution as it is articulated by one of its best advocates, Charles Hodge (though it also interacts with other important voices);[1] second, it discusses and evaluates some of the objections that are commonly raised against it; and third, it offers a critique of the applications of the doctrine that are erroneous and reductionistic. As part of this critique, the paper will consider several insights from Dietrich Bonhoeffer.

2. *The Doctrine as Articulated by Charles Hodge*

According to Charles Hodge, the justice of God is the foundation for the plan of salvation that is revealed in the New Testament.[2] By this, Hodge means, first, that God is supremely holy and cannot maintain fellowship with unholy, sinful creatures.[3] Therefore, when human beings fell into sinful disobedience and corruption, they became alienated from their Creator. They descended from a state of moral perfection and holiness to a condition of total depravity. Second, God cannot simply pardon sin without a satisfaction of justice. It is God's nature to reward godly service and obedience, and to punish sin and disobedience.[4] Third, "man cannot satisfy the justice of God for himself, nor any creature for him . . ."[5] By their own efforts, people are totally impotent to satisfy God's just demands and thus achieve reconciliation and restoration to humanity's former glory and standing before God. As a result, humanity finds itself in the

1. Green and Baker also appeal to Hodge as an exemplary representative of the penal substitution view. See their *Recovering the Scandal of the Cross*, 142–50.

2. Hodge, *Systematic Theology*, 492.

3. Erickson explicitly states that his understanding of the atonement is based upon the assumption that the nature of God is perfect and complete holiness (*Christian Theology*, 802). Employing stronger language, Grudem argues that Christ's suffering on the cross was intensified due to the repugnance to his supreme holiness of the sin laid upon him: "Now Jesus was perfectly holy. He hated sin with his entire being . . . Taking on himself all the evil against which his soul rebelled created deep revulsion in the center of his being. All that he hated most deeply was poured out fully upon him" (*Systematic Theology*, 573).

4. Hodge, *Systematic Theology*, 489. Grudem says that "there is an eternal, unchangeable requirement in the holiness and justice of God that sin be paid for" (Grudem, *Systematic Theology*, 575).

5. Hodge, *Systematic Theology*, 481.

hopeless predicament of being rejected by and alienated from God. Its only hope for salvation lies in Jesus Christ, who alone can satisfy the just demands of God on humanity's behalf as its representative and substitute. Therefore, for Hodge, the gospel is the power of God unto salvation precisely because Christ's work *satisfies* the demands of God's justice.

The Nature of Christ's Satisfaction

Hodge presents three clarifying points to elucidate the nature of the atonement as a satisfaction. These are based on three key terms in his thesis: Christ's atoning work was a satisfaction in that it answered all of the demands of God's justice and God's law against the sinner. First, Christ's saving work was offered to satisfy God.[6] It was not offered primarily to affect a change in human beings, but to satisfy something intrinsic to the divine nature within God. This sacrifice was a perfect satisfaction, both in its efficacy and its applicability. It was efficacious because it completely satisfied God's just demands; it was applicable because Christ was a true representative of humanity. Therefore, there is no longer any basis for condemnation of sinners, for the demands of justice have been totally exhausted in Christ.[7] This is due not to the form and extent of his suffering, as if he suffered in kind and measure what sinners would have been required to suffer, but rather to the infinite dignity of his person, which gives his suffering an intrinsic worth. No mere creature, no abstract or distant deity, could accomplish this. For satisfaction to be applicable, it must be offered by a genuine human being; for it to be efficacious, it must be offered by a being of infinite merit and dignity (i.e., a divine being).[8] Only Jesus Christ, who is fully God and fully human, could offer such a satisfaction. Furthermore, the effects of Christ's satisfaction were both negative and positive, both passive and active. They were negative and passive in the sense that Christ suffered the punishment that

6. Hodge, *Systematic Theology*, 482.
7. Hodge, *Systematic Theology*, 483.
8. Hodge, *Systematic Theology*, 486.

belonged to sinners and paid their debt. They were positive and active in the sense that Christ accomplished for sinners what they could not accomplish for themselves, namely perfect righteousness and obedience to God. He both suffered in their place and offered his own righteousness to God on their behalf.[9] Hodge says, "It follows from this that the satisfaction of Christ has all the value which belongs to the obedience and sufferings of the eternal Son of God, and his righteousness, as well active as passive, is infinitely meritorious."[10]

Second, Christ's atoning work was offered to satisfy the demands of *God's justice*.[11] For Hodge, justice is not some abstract Platonic category to which God is subordinated. Rather, justice is intrinsic to God's nature and character, just as love is.[12] On this, all of the classical atonement theologies are agreed: God is just in defeating evil and Satan (Christus victor), in demonstrating to us the meaning of true justice, righteousness, and love (moral/exemplar), in securing a just pardon for sinners (forensic), or in punishing sin (penal substitution). What is distinctive about the penal substitution view is that God's justice is conceived not only as restorative (reforming sinners) or demonstrative (as a deterrent to sin), but also (often primarily) as retributive, distributive, and vindicatory.[13] Hodge explains:

> [God] is determined by his moral excellence to punish all sin, and therefore the satisfaction of Christ which secures the pardon of

9. See also Grudem's discussion of Christ's "active" and "passive" obedience; by the former Christ obeyed the regulations of the law for us and thus became our righteousness, while by the latter he suffered our penalty in our place (*Systematic Theology*, 570).

10. Hodge, *Systematic Theology*, 483.

11. Hodge, *Systematic Theology*, 489.

12. Hodge, *Systematic Theology*, 488–90. For Hodge, the key question is whether there is in God the attribute of retributive/distributive/vindicatory justice.

13. It is retributive in that God must punish sin simply because it is sin, regardless of whether or not such punishment will lead to reform or deterrence. It is distributive in that God responds to human actions with fairness and justice, impartially rewarding obedience and righteousness and punishing disobedience and unrighteousness. It is vindicatory in that God vindicates the righteous and opposes, frustrates, and even destroys the unrighteous.

> sinners is rendered to the justice of God. Its primary and principal design is neither to make a moral impression upon the offenders themselves, nor to operate didactically on other intelligent creatures, but to satisfy the demands of justice; so that God can be just in justifying the ungodly.[14]

However, Hodge also cautions his reader against mistaking God's vindicatory justice for vindictiveness or thirst for revenge.[15] The latter implies an irrational emotional response (as if God was personally demeaned or offended) while vindicatory justice implies simply those actions required by a just God.

Third, Christ's atoning work was offered to satisfy the demands of *God's law*.[16] Since this divine law is established by the nature and character of God, it is immutable and cannot simply be ignored or set aside.[17] According to Hodge, our relation to the law is both federal and moral. By "federal," Hodge means the soteriological function of the law to secure salvation under the covenant.[18] This "federal" law must be obeyed in its entirety, including both its prescriptions and its prohibitions. Transgression of the law in even the smallest detail amounts to absolute guilt, which results in condemnation and death. To effect salvation in human beings, Christ satisfies the law of God, not by abolishing it or even by lowering its demands, but by fulfilling it completely on their behalf (as their representative) and in their place (as their substitute). This fulfillment of the law on behalf of sinners does not lead to antinomianism, as if there is no longer

14. Hodge, *Systematic Theology*, 493.

15. However, Grudem comes very close to this (if not endorsing it) when he says, "Jesus became the object of the intense hatred of sin and vengeance against sin which God had patiently stored up since the beginning of the world" (*Systematic Theology*, 575).

16. Hodge, *Systematic Theology*, 493.

17. One might well ask of Hodge whether retributive action is the only way to "satisfy" God's law.

18. Paul Wells ("Free Lunch," 48), following F. Turretin, explains that in Reformed covenantal theology the law has three applications, including moral (universal, natural law), federal (covenantal, binding humanity to God), and penal (exacts punishment on sinners).

any place for the law in the lives of believers. For, while Christ delivers people from the law's federal requirements, he does not thereby remove or destroy its moral significance.[19] In other words, obeying the law still has moral and practical value, but such obedience is no longer required for salvation. Believers access the saving benefits achieved by Christ through faith, while those who reject Christ are still under the federal requirements of the law.

How Does Christ Achieve Satisfaction?

So far, we have examined Hodge's explanation of what Christ does to secure our salvation. Next, we explore Hodge's account of how Christ does it. First, Christ saves us as our priest.[20] A priest is someone who goes before God on behalf of the people as a representative. As such, the priest intercedes for the people, acting on their behalf in the presence of God. The priest also acts on behalf of God in the presence of the people, mediating God's presence and actions toward them. According to Hodge, Christ's priesthood must be understood in light of the Old Testament sacrificial system, in which the forgiveness of sins could only be effected by means of expiation through the shedding of blood. Such expiation, according to Hodge, was accomplished by substituting a victim in place of the sinner. Since the removal of guilt required punishment, the guilt of the sinner was transferred to a victim that was sacrificed in the sinner's place.[21] This expiation covered the guilt of the sinner, hiding it from the sight of God. Expiation should not be confused with reconciliation, rather the latter should be regarded as an effect of the former.[22]

Second, Christ saves us not only as our priest but also as our sacrifice. He becomes simultaneously the one who offers and the offering itself. Furthermore, since his sacrifice must fulfill the

19. Hodge, *Systematic Theology*, 493.

20. Hodge, *Systematic Theology*, 496.

21. See also Erickson, who argues that Old Testament sacrifices atoned for sins by means of vicarious punishment, not by reforming the sinner or by social deterrence (*Christian Theology*, 804). However, Peter Schmiechen denies that sacrifices function in a vicarious or substitutionary way (*Saving Power*, 111).

22. Hodge, *Systematic Theology*, 497.

requirements of God's retributive justice, it must be offered as a propitiation to satisfy God's wrath.[23] Hodge argues that this propitiation *is secured by the expiation (removal) of guilt*, so that sin no longer appears before God as demanding punishment. The effect of this sin offering, therefore, is that sinners are pardoned and restored to God's favor. It is almost as though God's wrath, being stirred by and tied to the presence of sin, is turned away by expiation, which removes sin from God's sight. Thus, at first glance, it seems that, for Hodge, expiation (as the removal of sin) is more dominant than the theme of punishment. However, Hodge goes on to say that expiation *is effected by vicarious punishment*. Thus, while propitiation is secured by expiation, expiation is in turn accomplished by the vicarious punishment of a victim in place of an offender. That this latter theme of vicarious punishment predominates Hodge's view becomes obvious as his discussion unfolds. He makes it clear that sin offerings for the expiation of sin were "not designed proximately for the reformation of the offender, but to secure the remission of the *penalty* due to his transgressions" (emphasis mine).[24] For Hodge, Christ satisfies God by offering himself as a propitiation for sinners, a sacrifice which expiates sin by vicariously bearing its punishment.[25]

23. Hodge, *Systematic Theology*, 499.

24. To support his point, Hodge appeals to ceremonies in the Old Testament sacrificial cult. First, victims were selected from the clean class of animals and were free from blemish. Second, the offender was required to bring the victim to the altar. Third, the hands of the offender were laid on the head of the victim, symbolizing the transfer of guilt from the former to the latter. Fourth, the victim's blood was sprinkled on the altar or, on the Day of Atonement, carried into the Most Holy Place and sprinkled on the ark of the covenant, symbolizing that the offering was meant to propitiate God. See also Erickson, who argues that atoning sacrifices were intended to appease God's justice by offering a victim to bear guilt and suffer punishment in place of the sinner (*Christian Theology*, 805).

25. Hodge, *Systematic Theology*, 506–10. Hodge points to several passages for support of his view, including Isaiah 53, Rom 3:25; 8:3; Gal 1:4; Heb 9:14; and 2 Cor 5:21.

Third, Christ saves us as our redeemer. Redemption, for Hodge, means "deliverance from evil by the payment of a ransom."[26] The main point of the ransom metaphor is that sinners are in bondage and in need of deliverance. Clearly, the payment rendered to redeem sinners was Christ himself, in particular his death on the cross. However, Hodge believes that speculation about to whom the ransom was paid pushes the metaphor too far. For example, he rejects the view, held by some of the early Fathers, that God pays a ransom to Satan.[27]

Thus, the focus of the metaphor is not on the creditor, but on the debtors and the payment offered for their redemption. Furthermore, the ransom or redemption metaphor does not operate in isolation, but in interdependence with the penal substitution theory. Redemption is effected by Christ's atoning work in bearing our punishment. Hodge elucidates this relationship in his discussion of the ways in which redemption brings freedom to those formerly in bondage. First, it frees them from the penalty of the law, which is the wrath and curse of God directed against transgressors.[28] Christ frees transgressors from this penalty by suffering punishment in their place. Second, it frees them from their obligation to satisfy perfectly the demands of the law.[29] In particular, they are freed from its federal demands. While the law still plays a moral function in the lives of believers (i.e., for the enrichment of life), it no longer determines their eternal destiny. Third, Christ's redemption frees people from the power of sin. Hodge affirms that "He gave Himself that He might purify unto Himself a peculiar people zealous of good works."[30] Having been restored to the favor of God, the believer's soul is now vivified by the love of God and is restored in the image of God. Thus, the power of sin over the believer is defeated (though this happens gradually through sanctification). Fourth, redemption

26. Hodge, *Systematic Theology*, 516.
27. Hodge, *Systematic Theology*, 565.
28. Hodge, *Systematic Theology*, 516.
29. Hodge, *Systematic Theology*, 517.
30. Hodge, *Systematic Theology*, 518.

frees people from the power of Satan.[31] According to Hodge, Satan, as the accuser, has the office of inflicting the penalty of the law, to which all people (as sinners) are subject. When Christ satisfied the penalty of the law by his sacrificial death, he thus stripped Satan of his power over believers.[32] Christ did not annihilate the devil by dying on the cross, but he did disarm him by disabling the primary weapons of his arsenal (i.e., accusation, condemnation, despair, and punishment based on the demands of the law). Finally, Christ's redemptive work ultimately frees people from all evil. While evil is a consequence of the fall, of the curse resulting from violation of the law, redemption overturns the curse and thus implies being delivered from all evil.

Summary of Principles

Before we move to the next point, a summary of Hodge's penal substitution theory is in order. First, justice is the starting point.[33] God is absolutely holy and cannot abide the presence of sin. Second, humanity is in a state of total depravity, which means not that humans are as bad as they possibly could be, but that humans are infected with sin to the depths of their being and are totally unable to satisfy God's just demands and thus effect their own salvation. Third, fallenness is regarded primarily as a state of guilt, which leads to condemnation and alienation, while salvation is regarded primarily as satisfying justice, which leads to a restoration of favor and relationship. Fourth, since people cannot achieve their own salvation, they are in need of a representative and substitute to achieve it on their behalf and in their place. To be genuine, a representative must be fully human; to be efficacious, a substitute must be fully God. Thus, fifth, the Incarnation is conceived of as a necessary step in God's solution for dealing with human sin. Christ, as fully God and fully man, is

31. Hodge, *Systematic Theology*, 518–19.

32. Hodge, *Systematic Theology*, 565.

33. Green and Baker concur that at the heart of Hodge's explanation of the atonement is a legal metaphor that is indebted to his understanding of the criminal justice system of his time (*Recovering the Scandal of the Cross*, 146).

both a genuine representative and an efficacious substitute for humanity. Sixth, Christ satisfies God's justice and God's law for sinners, on their behalf and in their place, as their priest, sacrifice, and redeemer. Finally, Hodge believes that the penal substitution view accommodates the themes addressed by the other major atonement metaphors.

3. *Objections and Responses to Critics*

Objections raised against the penal substitution view typically fall into one of two categories, namely ethical objections and theological objections. In this section, I briefly explore these objections along with the responses given by proponents of penal substitution.

Ethical Objections

One ethical objection commonly raised is that sin and guilt are personal and non-transferable.[34] It is both inappropriate and unfair for God to satisfy justice by punishing an innocent person (Christ) in place of guilty offenders. Erickson and Grudem respond by emphasizing the fact that Christ's suffering was voluntarily, that Christ willingly offered his life on behalf of sinners.[35] This response is partially helpful in that it presents Christ as a willing participant, but it does not show how punishing an innocent person serves the cause of justice itself. How is it just to add evil to evil? Does not the death of Christ create a further injustice? Grudem is not very helpful when he responds:

> God himself (Father, Son, and Holy Spirit) is the ultimate standard of what is just and fair in the universe, and he decreed that the atonement would take place in this way, and that it did in fact satisfy the demands of his own righteousness and justice.[36]

Apparently for Grudem, justice is served because God says so (apparently in good nominalist fashion). God determines what

34. Wells, "Free Lunch," 43.
35. Grudem, *Systematic Theology*, 574; Erickson, *Christian Theology*, 817.
36. Grudem, *Systematic Theology*, 574.

is just and may therefore turn evil into good simply by declaring it to be so. But if this is the case, why cannot God simply declare all sin to be forgiven? Perhaps a better response to this charge is that justice is served because Christ is, in some sense, *actually guilty*. Not that Christ ever *committed* sin, but in the Incarnation and atonement he united himself to sinful human beings and thus, in a mysterious yet real way, he became "guilty" for us in order to make us righteous. He identified with us, in order to incorporate us into union with himself and thus into deep fellowship with the triune God.[37] As Paul writes, "God made him who had no sin *to be sin for us*, so that in him we might become the righteousness of God" (2 Cor 5:21; emphasis added). Hans Boersma articulates this view clearly:

> Since God assumes the penalty rather than punishing a third party, God can no longer be construed as a "bloodthirsty" God who punishes the innocent. Rather, by absorbing the punishment and thus enabling humankind to obtain forgiveness, God offers hope for the attainment of ultimate justice.[38]

A related objection to the penal substitution view is that Christ cannot fulfill the law or the righteous demands of God for us. It is not possible for one person to "be good" in place of someone else. Erickson responds that the atonement is not an "arms-length transaction," but that we are united to Christ in his death and resurrection.[39] Hans Boersma, who defends the penal substitution view, admits that it is often portrayed (especially in more popular evangelical theology) as "a strict economy of exchange: the covenantal relationship between God and human

37. The language of "identification for incorporation" comes from McKnight (*Community Called Atonement*, 107–14).

38. Boersma, "Eschatological Justice," 198.

39. Erickson, *Christian Theology*, 818. However, his qualification that our union with Christ is "in the sight of God" weakens his position. While he wants to get beyond a mere transaction to a deeper union, this qualifying phrase seems to be a regression back to the former. Is the believer *actually* united with Christ or not? Erickson does not clarify this point.

beings takes on strongly contractual connotations."[40] This tends to happen especially when the penal view is articulated in isolation from the other atonement metaphors. Boersma suggests that the solution is a blend of the penal view with the recapitulation theory of Irenaeus.[41] He argues that Irenaeus connects the Incarnation with eschatological justice by viewing the atoning work of Christ as a recapitulation of Adam's creation, life, and death. In the Incarnation, Christ enters into a mystical union with humanity, in order to destroy human sin in his own flesh by his death on the cross. In the same way, Christ's union with humanity means that his resurrection from the dead creates the possibility for new life for human beings. By means of his union with humanity, Christ bears our punishment and fulfills the demands of righteousness for us. Those who are *in Christ* have died with him and are raised to new life through faith in him. What happened to Christ happens also to them.

A third ethical objection is that the penal substitution view celebrates and justifies redemptive violence as a solution to human problems. God the Father satisfies the demands of justice by inflicting upon the Son unthinkable, torturous violence—in fact, "the most horrible and contemptuous form of execution known to the ancient world."[42] Critics have referred to penal substitution as a theory of "cosmic child abuse" committed by a "sadistic and bloodthirsty" God.[43] Furthermore, critics have

40. Boersma, "Penal Substitution," 92.

41. Boersma, "Eschatological Justice," 194–95. See as well McKnight, who also appeals to themes of recapitulation and union with Christ. His overriding proposal is the atonement as "identification for incorporation," in which Jesus as the incarnate Son of God identifies fully with human beings in order to incorporate them into union with himself, and thus union (via reconciliation) with God and each other (*Community Called Atonement*, 54–69, 100–106, 107–14). McKnight argues that understanding the atonement as "identification for incorporation" allows us to incorporate several atonement metaphors, including recapitulation, ransom, Christus victor, satisfaction, substitution, representation, penal substitution, and moral exemplar. I am inclined to agree with him.

42. Marshall, "The Death of Jesus," 13.

43. Brock, *Journeys by Heart*, 56; Crysdale, *Embracing Travail*, 115. McKnight rejects such criticisms as being too simplistic, and because they lift writers and their thoughts out of context. Nevertheless, he goes on to urge

charged that such a view of the atonement has disastrous social implications:

> The images are particularly harmful for people who live in oppressive situations—a woman who is abused by her husband, or a people living under military occupation and whose land is being stolen daily by the occupiers. If these people are told to "be like Jesus," it is an invitation for them to follow Jesus' example of submitting passively to unmerited suffering because the ruler wants it.[44]

Hans Boersma has written a convincing response to such criticisms.[45] First, punishment and crime are fundamentally different categories; one cannot employ the former to justify the latter.[46] Punishment may only be enforced by legitimate authorities. In the penal substitution view, God (and only God) is in a position of such authority, hence God's punishment is just. Therefore, one cannot justify violent crimes by appealing to divine penal justice. That would amount to a serious category error: "Penal substitution . . . takes us into the realm of punishment, not into the realm of crime."[47] Second, the rejection of

defenders of penal substitution to exercise greater care in articulating what they mean, in part by distancing themselves from crassly caricatured misunderstandings (i.e., those depicting an angry God venting his rage on his Son). See *Community Called Atonement*, 41–42.

44. Weaver, "The Violence of Satisfaction."

45. Elsewhere, Boersma makes the point that critics who reject the penal satisfaction view because of its violence, in favor of other atonement metaphors, fail to see that *every view of the atonement* somehow associates God with violence. In the Christus victor model, God either deceived the devil (does violence to truth) or conquers him by outright military conquest (Boersma notes that Constantine drew on the Christus victor tradition to support his imperial power). The Abelardian moral influence theory also involves violence, because God enacts or allows the sacrifice of his Son in order to demonstrate his love to the world (Boersma, "Penal Substitution," 89–91). For Boersma, the use of violence in and of itself is not the primary issue (violence cannot be avoided unless God has nothing whatsoever to do with the cross); the fundamental question is whether a particular instance of violence is justified and appropriate.

46. Boersma, "Eschatological Justice," 188–89.

47. Boersma, "Eschatological Justice," 188.

all penal aspects of justice would actually lead to an increase, not a decrease, in violence.[48] Without recourse to punishment, a society would degenerate into anarchy. Punishment can be useful as a deterrent to prevent violence from occurring in greater degree and frequency. In addition, without recourse to penal justice, the victims of crime would be left in a state of frustration and powerlessness. They might even decide to take vengeance into their own hands, or else others might take up a vigilante cause on their behalf. Conversely, Christians are exhorted to relinquish revenge and retribution, not because such retribution is inherently unjust, but because vengeance belongs to God who alone can be trusted to vindicate the righteous and punish the oppressor properly. Third, those who attack the penal substitution view as glorifying violence fail to see that punishment is God's last option and is usually only enforced after continued warning or even pleading for people to repent. In light of this insight, Boersma likens the penal dimension of the cross to God's use of exile to punish Israel: "It is certainly true that God would rather forgive than punish, often does forgive rather than punish . . . But the biblical narrative highlights Israel's consistent rejection of God's plans for justice. Exile seeks to subvert this constant pattern."[49] Fourth, viewing penal substitution in light of the Incarnation shows that God has taken judgment upon himself.[50] Or, as Erickson puts it, "Christ was sent by the *Father's* love. So it is not the case that the propitiation changed a wrathful God into a loving God."[51] Rather, the wrathful God *is* loving. Or, as Luther argued, God's wrath is an instrument of God's love:[52]

48. Boersma, "Eschatological Justice," 190–92.

49. Boersma, "Eschatological Justice," 193–94.

50. Boersma, "Eschatological Justice," 198.

51. Erickson, *Christian Theology*, 817.

52. Green and Baker argue that God's grace outlasts God's wrath, because grace is foundational to God's character while wrath is temporary and contextual (*Recovering the Scandal of the Cross*, 51–53).

> "For love's anger (wrath) seeks and wills to sunder the evil that it hates from the good that it loves, in order that the good and its love may be preserved."
> "Wrath is truly God's alien work, which He employs contrary to His nature because He is forced into it by the wickedness of man."[53]

Theological Objections

While several theological objections could be raised, I will focus on three of the more prominent ones. The first two are less convincing, while the third is more serious. First, some critics argue that the penal substitution view is anti-Trinitarian.[54] The idea that God the Father punishes the Son for human sin amounts to a tri-theistic division of the Trinity and introduces contradictory or schizophrenic motivations into the godhead (i.e., the Son is loving and self-sacrificing, while the Father is vindictive and requires placation). However, while popular portrayals sometimes lean toward this depiction, they represent a fundamental misunderstanding of penal substitution.[55] The view in question does not pit the Son against the Father or the Father against the Son. Rather, both Father and Son are motivated by their love for human beings and both Father and Son want to eradicate sin and evil in the world. Both want to ensure forgiveness and restoration while simultaneously upholding justice. They simply play different roles in the outworking of salvation. In support of this delicate tension, an oft-quoted verse is 2 Cor 5:19: "In Christ, God was reconciling the world to himself." How? Verse 21

53. Quoted from Ngien, *The Suffering of God*, 107. Ngien comments, "The 'wrathful' opposition against 'sin' is not generated by some abstractly conceived justice of God, which demands retribution for the broken law; rather it is generated by God's 'pure love' which demands a pure, simple and undefiled relationship."

54. Wells, "Free Lunch," 43. See also Schmiechen, *Saving Power*, 112–13.

55. For example, Leon Morris, a proponent of the penal satisfaction view, states explicitly: "Salvation is not something wrung from an unwilling God by the desperate intervention of a compassionate Son who took pity on those subject to the Father's destroying wrath. Salvation proceeds rather from the loving heart of God the Father Himself. It is an expression at once of His love and of His righteousness" (Morris, *The Cross in the New Testament*, 154).

continues, "For our sake he made him to be sin who knew no sin, so that in him we might become the righteousness of God."

A second theological objection concerns the nature and function of sacrifice. The penal substitution view claims support from the Old Testament sacrificial system, seeing it as a key to interpreting the sacrifice of Christ. In particular, the view relies on the interpretation of the sacrifices as propitiatory offerings, intended to satisfy God's wrath against sin. Sacrifices, in this view, were offered on behalf of sinners and in their place (they were representative and substitutive). Hodge claims that Old Testament sin offerings were for the expiation of sin, which secured propitiation by the remission of the penalty or punishment due to transgression of the law.[56] On the basis of his understanding of words like "propitiation" and "sacrifice" in Scripture, Leon Morris argues that the entire New Testament makes sense only "on the basis that God sent His Son to die on the cross and so made a way of forgiveness for sinners."[57] For Morris, when the New Testament speaks of Christ's death as propitiation, it unmistakably means that "Christ's death is the way in which God's wrath is averted from man" and without it "there is nothing to show how the wrath is turned away."[58]

However, Peter Schmiechen argues that "the idea of satisfaction or appeasement of God is simply not biblical."[59] He explains that "(1) the entire system of sin offerings was instituted by God for the remission of sin; (2) that the offering was to cover or remove sin; (3) that it was not directed toward God as a form of appeasement."[60] Furthermore, he argues that the smearing of animal blood on the sacrificial alter was effective because the life-bearing blood of the animal, not its death, resulted in a change. It symbolized the covering of sin, such that sin was removed from God's sight. Sacrifice was directed toward sin to

56. Hodge, *Systematic Theology*, 503.

57. Morris, *The Cross of Jesus*, 5.

58. Morris, *The Cross of Jesus*, 226. For a detailed account of the meaning of propitiation, see Morris's, *The Apostolic Preaching of the Cross* (esp. chs. 4–5).

59. Schmiechen, *Saving Power*, 111.

60. Schmiechen, *Saving Power*, 111. See also 20–55.

effect purification, not toward God to effect appeasement.[61] Hence, the primary idea behind sacrifice is "expiation" (removal of sin), not propitiation (substitution to appease God's wrath).[62] Schmiechen raises a good point, which should challenge defenders of penal substitution and divine retributive justice (at the very least) to nuance their position more carefully. The writer of the book of Hebrews seems to confirm Schmiechen's emphasis on atonement as purification and removal of sin through Christ's righteousness, rather than as the appeasement of wrath through punishment. It is Christ's righteousness and obedience that "appeases" God, not his torturous suffering. Consider, for example, the following passages:

> Every high priest chosen from among mortals is put in charge of things pertaining to God on their behalf, to offer gifts and sacrifices for sins.
>
> In the days of his flesh, Jesus offered up prayers and supplications, with loud cries and tears, to the one who was able to save him from death, and he was heard because of his reverent submission. Although he was a Son, he learned obedience through what he suffered; and having been made perfect, he became the source of eternal salvation for all who obey him.
>
> [Christ] has become a priest . . . through the power of an indestructible life.[63]

On the other hand, Schmiechen does not, to my satisfaction, address texts that mention God's wrath against sin explicitly and how Christ's atoning work attends to it (e.g., Rom 5:9–10; 8:3–4; Col 3:6).[64] His position would be strengthened if he clarified

61. Schmiechen, *Saving Power*, 22. Similarly, Schmiechen argues that the scapegoat on the Day of Atonement symbolized purification or removal of sin. While sins are transferred to the scapegoat, the victim does not die vicariously for sinners as a substitute for their death penalty.

62. Conversely, Wells (citing Morris): argues that "when Scripture uses the word 'blood,' in almost all cases it indicates not the life of the animal, but its death" ("Free Lunch," 49).

63. Heb 5:1, 7–9; 7:16.

64. McKnight affirms that the notion of penal substitution is present in the New Testament, though it should not be over-emphasized or made primary

and specified the nature, purpose, object, and resolution of this "wrath". In any case, it is unlikely that this debate will be resolved soon. Until it is, I am persuaded of the correctness of Hodge's view, which integrates both expiation and propitiation as key elements of atoning sacrifice. I. Howard Marshall supports this position:

> If the sacrifice is regarded as expiatory in the sense that it cancels out the effect of sin, it does so in that it propitiates God against whom the sin was committed; and equally, if it is regarded as propitiating God, it does so by covering the sin which aroused his judgment. Expiation and propitiation are two sides of the same coin.[65]

A third theological objection is that penal substitution prioritizes justice over all other divine attributes. As Schmiechen comments regarding Hodge's system, "it is the demand of legal justice that drives the entire theory."[66] Again, "The Law of distributive justice is immutable."[67] Hans Boersma also notices the tendency in popular portrayals of penal substitution to separate God's justice and mercy, or even to valorize the former over the latter. The God depicted by such portrayals is understandably perceived as being "bloodthirsty." Likewise, the designation of the atonement as a "satisfaction," if it is not carefully nuanced and enriched by other metaphors, often becomes fixated upon divine wrath and "obscures the all-encompassing love of God."[68] However, skilful proponents of the penal substitution view, such as Hodge and Boersma, are careful to avoid such implications. For example, Hodge clarifies that justice is not a law that transcends God, one to which God is somehow subordinate. Nor does the idea of divine justice imply necessity or determinism in God, as if God must act according to an impersonal mechanism. Rather, retributive justice is inherent to God's character; it is a

over other scriptural concepts and images concerning sin and atonement (*Community Called Atonement*, 107–14).

65. Marshall, "The Death of Jesus," 16.
66. Schmiechen, *Saving Power*, 103.
67. Schmiechen, *Saving Power*, 110.
68. Boersma, "Eschatological Justice," 187.

natural expression of the nature and being of God to act justly.[69] In other words, justice is not God, but *God is just*. The same argument applies to God's love. Some critics dismiss outright the notion of divine retribution as inherently demeaning to God and argue instead (or at least imply) that love determines God's essence. In other words, they introduce a necessity to love by assuming that God *must always* act lovingly. Is not this assertion equally open to the charge of necessity or determinism? Of course, the proper response is that love, like justice, is inherent to God's character. Love is not God, but *God is loving*. In both cases, it is the character of God that defines for us the genuine meaning of genuine justice and love. Having acknowledged this, we are left with this question: Why does Hodge prioritize justice over love, making it the foundation for his system? (One might further ask whether Hodge actually prioritizes *his own presuppositions about what constitutes justice* over God's love.)[70] I propose that this a legitimate weakness of the penal substitution view. As Schmiechen has suggested, the penal substitution view tends to resolve the tension between justice and love by prioritizing the former over the latter and making it the determinative principle of the atonement.[71] This is highly problematic, biblically, theologically, ethically, and missionally.[72]

69. Hodge, *Systematic Theology*, 489. Green and Baker seem to misread Hodge on this point (see *Recovering the Scandal of the Cross*, 147).

70. See Green and Baker, *Recovering the Scandal of the Cross*, 146. They contrast Hodge's view of justice, which borrows from both Anselm and late nineteenth-century American notions of justice, with a "biblical understanding of justice that is covenantal and relational and almost synonymous with faithfulness" (p. 147).

71. Schmiechen, *Saving Power*, 110.

72. Where one begins is, of course, crucially important. As McKnight puts it, "*where we begin* shapes *where we end up*. If you begin with wrath, you get an atonement that tells the story of wrath being pacified" (*Community Called Atonement*, 15, emphasis his)

4. *The Real Problem: Reductionism*

In my view, the best approach to the atonement is to recognize the validity and significance of all of the biblical atonement metaphors.[73] The saving work of Christ affects people to the very depths of their being and personhood. It impacts them spiritually, relationally, psychologically, epistemologically, ethically, and even physically.[74] Moreover, it affects not just individuals, but also families, communities, societies, power structures, the environment, and even cosmic forces (Gen 12:3; Matt 5–7; Acts 1:6–8; 10:34–35, 44–48; Col 1:15–20; etc.).[75] Each of the atonement metaphors highlights different aspects of Christ's saving work, and none comprehensively addresses them all. Each metaphor is important because the eternal truth of Christ's death has particular relevance to people in particular circumstances. As Leon Morris has argued, "we experience needs of our own for which the cross gives an answer."[76] Thus, what is needed is an approach that allows the various atonement metaphors to coexist in a kind of perichoretic union—one in which the distinctiveness of each view is maintained even while it contributes to a unified (but not uniform) understanding of salvation.[77]

73. Green and Baker (*Recovering the Scandal of the Cross*, 23) identify five primary constellations of atonement images in the New Testament, all borrowed from the ancient Mediterranean world. These include: (i) the court of law (e.g., justification); (ii) the world of commerce (e.g., redemption); (iii) personal relationships (e.g., reconciliation); (iv) worship (e.g., sacrifice); and (v) the battleground (e.g., triumph over evil).

74. Granted, the experience of complete salvation is an already-not-yet eschatological process, in which some aspects are experienced in the present, others in the near future, and perhaps still others in the eschaton.

75. For some creative insights regarding the significance of the atonement for a wide range of issues affecting the human condition, see Morris, *The Cross of Jesus* (esp. chs. 3–7).

76. Morris, *The Cross of Jesus*, viii.

77. Morris, *The Cross of Jesus*, recommends a "multi-faceted" approach; Green, "Kaleidoscopic View," argues for a "kaleidoscope" approach; van Asselt ("Christ's Atonement") envisions a "multi-dimensional" approach; and McKnight (*Community Called Atonement*) suggests "identification for incurporation" as a framework in which all of the atonement metaphors find an

The penal substitution view, as articulated by Hodge, is a helpful solution to the problems of human disobedience, culpability in sin, or participation in radical and inexplicable evil. It is therefore an apt and poignant expression of the gospel to people who are burdened with feelings of guilt (or, conversely, those who are puffed up with pride).[78] It is, perhaps, not as helpful for those whose predominant experience of their fallen human condition comes in the form of loneliness, aimlessness, or despair at the injustices they observe in the world. The penal substitution view does communicate important truths about God and the human condition, but it must be applied properly with due consideration given to context or audience. Unfortunately, it is often the case that when the penal substitution theory is articulated and applied, two errors are commonly made (especially in popular portrayals). Both errors fall under the category of reductionism; hence, both compromise the richness of a multi-dimensional approach to the atonement and threaten to undermine and dismantle its delicate unity-in-diversity.

Penal Substitution as a Metanarrative

The first error commonly made is to grant the penal substitution metaphor the status of a metanarrative. A metanarrative is a grand story, which claims to account for all of the facts by subsuming them into and arranging them under one dominant theme, idea, principle, or system. In recent times, metanarratives have become suspect. In particular, postmodern theorists have pointed out their tendency to suppress otherness, difference, and complexity. Metanarratives tell a dominant story, or support a dominant ideology, philosophy, or theology, by silencing or downplaying other views. They achieve unity and clarity by

appropriate place. Boersma's position is that the penal satisfaction view needs to be grounded in such a way that it does not favor God's justice over his love, and perhaps is included within a larger framework of union with Christ with reference to the recapitulation theory of Irenaeus (See Boersma, "Eschatological Justice," 194–97).

78. In fact, the penal substitution view is the only atonement metaphor that specifically addresses the problem of human guilt.

erasing distinctiveness and counterclaims. For example, one metanarrative that has harmed modern Christian faith is scientism or natural reductionism. In this grand story of modern science, something can only be considered true if it can be proved scientifically by empirical evidence. This view is reductionistic because scientific inquiry cannot account for the complexity of reality. It cannot explain things like art, music, love, justice, faith, and hope, in a way that is fully meaningful for people.[79]

Similarly, penal substitution takes on the character of a metanarrative when it is portrayed as the whole Christian story (or at least the part that really matters) and is virtually equated with "the gospel." When this happens, other important truths about the gospel (arguably more central ones) are ignored, including such things as costly discipleship, the kingdom of God (which Jesus always linked with "the gospel"), and the overcoming of evil and suffering in the world. In North America, the use of penal substitution as a metanarrative has tended to reinforce a bland Christianity, which is theologically shallow, individualistic, self-centered, and ethically ambiguous (a strange blend of legalism regarding personal piety or holiness and antinomianism or carelessness regarding issues of structural evil and social justice).[80] Furthermore, it has tended to address only one aspect of the experience of the fallen human condition, namely guilt. Consequently, it has preached an increasingly irrelevant message, which has had the effect of turning the good news into old news.[81] In addition, a fixation on penal substitution has alienated people whose deep needs are more aptly addressed by other aspects of the atonement. Christ's atoning work is bountifully rich, exceedingly comprehensive, and powerfully efficacious. Why limit it to a narrow and individualistic invitation to receive

79. For a further critique of natural reductionism in science, see Peterson, *Genetic Turning Points*, 32.

80. Regarding the individualism and self-centeredness of North American culture, see also Green and Baker, *Recovering the Scandal of the Cross*, 24–25, 150, 201, 213–14.

81. See also Green and Baker, *Recovering the Scandal of the Cross*, 29–30.

the forgiveness of sins in order to secure one's personal salvation? (Again, I want to stress that these concerns are important, but they are far from being the whole story, or even the primary plot). As Dietrich Bonhoeffer once reflected,

> Hasn't the individualistic question about personal salvation almost completely left us all? Aren't we really under the impression that there are more important things than that question (perhaps not more important than the *matter* itself, but more important than the *question*!)? . . . Does the question about saving one's soul appear in the Old Testament at all? Aren't righteousness and the Kingdom of God on earth the focus of everything, and isn't it true that Rom. 3.24ff. is not an individualistic doctrine of salvation, but the culmination of the view that God alone is righteous? It is not with the beyond that we are concerned, but with this world as created and preserved, subjected to laws, reconciled, and restored. What is above this world is, in the gospel, intended to exist *for* this world; I mean that, not in the anthropocentric sense of liberal, mystic pietistic, ethical theology, but in the biblical sense of the creation and of the incarnation, crucifixion, and resurrection of Jesus Christ.[82]

One way to avoid making the penal substitution view into a metanarrative is to resist the tendency to interpret it too literally. When I say this, I am not suggesting that we become suspicious of its truthfulness, or take it less seriously. I am simply suggesting that we accept it for what it is—a metaphor (even if a divinely inspired one). Like any metaphor, it bears both continuity and discontinuity with what it seeks to represent, and one must be careful not to push its limits too far. All metaphors break down if pushed too far; worse, they actually become *literal* and lose their creative metaphorical power. As Colin Gunton reminds us, "the truth of a claim about the world does not depend on whether it is expressed in literal or metaphorical terms, but upon whether language of whatever kind expresses human interaction with reality successfully (truthfully) or not."[83] Literalizing a metaphor emasculates the truth it was meant to communicate.

82. Bonhoeffer, *Letters and Papers*, 285–86.
83. Gunton, *Actuality of Atonement*, 35.

Discerning the limits of the penal substitution view will require a good deal of reflection as well as sensitivity to cultural context and the needs of people. Such reflection is not easy, but it is necessary.[84] Actually, we commonly do the same thing when we explain the ransom theory. When the following question is asked of the ransom theory, "To whom is the ransom paid?", the common response is that such a question pushes the ransom metaphor too far. All that can be said is that the atonement is a ransom in the sense that Christ's sacrifice redeems us "in some way" from debt to sin and bondage to evil. Perhaps it is possible to speak of the penal substitution view in like manner. Perhaps all that we can and should say is that Christ's atoning work saves us by satisfying the justice of God "in some way."[85]

Penal Substitution as a Methodology

The second error often made in the application of the penal substitution metaphor is when it is turned into a methodology for evangelism.[86] This practice is commonplace in North America, hence two examples will suffice. One example is the way in which many people define a "gospel sermon" or a "gospel message." Typically, the expectation is that a gospel message

84. Green and Baker, *Recovering the Scandal of the Cross*, 20–21, insightfully write, "As is often the case in our use of the New Testament, our use of tradition often falters because we learn less *how* the theological task has been undertaken and exemplified, and attempt instead to carry over into our own lives and pronouncements models and metaphors that belong to another age and that are dead to us. Metaphors work within cultures where a shared encyclopedia can be assumed. Crossing cultures requires the creation of new metaphors, new ways of conceptualizing and communicating. Often to the detriment of fidelity in understanding do we borrow metaphors from other cultures and use them as if they were our own."

85. Gunton writes, "excessive preoccupation with the juridical aspects of the doctrine of justification has led to versions of penal substitution which do appear to attribute to God an excessively punitive character. So much hangs on a sensitive appreciation of what are the possibilities and limits of the legal metaphor" (*Actuality of Atonement*, 101).

86. For a related discussion, see Green and Baker's insightful distinction between "technique" and "craft," which they borrow from Alasdair MacIntyre (*Recovering the Scandal of the Cross*, 214–17).

will provide a step-by-step account of the penal substitution view of the atonement (which is virtually equated with the gospel), followed by an opportunity to "accept Christ." Usually, such messages are preached without any reference to the other atonement metaphors. A second example is the wide-spread use of the so-called "Four Spiritual Laws" in evangelism, which are explicitly derived from the penal view. In such evangelistic encounters, people are led through a series of propositions that tell them that God, while loving, is absolutely holy and righteous, that all people are sinners, that the consequence of sin is death, but that Christ offers forgiveness freely to those who "accept" him in faith as their Savior.[87] Again, rarely is any mention made of the other atonement views. Furthermore, when combined with the North American context of individualism and consumerism, such "invitations" rarely make costly demands on potential converts.

There are at least two problems with this kind of methodological reductionism. First, it promotes what Dietrich Bonhoeffer called "cheap grace."[88] It tends to present salvation as a mechanistic transaction between God and sinner, one in which God makes no demands and yet pays for all the benefits. Bonhoeffer defines cheap grace as follows:

> Cheap grace means grace as bargain-basement goods, cut-rate forgiveness, cut-rate comfort, cut-rate sacrament; grace as the church's inexhaustible pantry, from which it is doled out by careless hands without hesitation or limit. It is grace without a price, without costs.

87. There are many Internet sites that explain the Four Spiritual Laws. See, for example: http://powertochange.com/landing/four-laws/. The Four Spiritual Laws are: "1. God loves you and offers a wonderful plan for your life; 2. All of us are sinful and separated from God. Therefore, we cannot know and experience God's love and plan for our life; 3. Jesus Christ is God's only provision for our sin. Through him, we can know and experience God's love and plan for our life; 4. We must individually accept Jesus Christ as Savior and Lord; then, we can know and experience God's love and plan for our life." (Accessed April 4, 2009). It is instructive to compare these Four Laws with my summary of Hodge's position on pp. 30–31.

88. Bonhoeffer, *Discipleship*, 43–56.

> Cheap grace means grace as doctrine, as principle, as system. It means forgiveness of sins as a general truth; it means God's love as merely a Christian idea of God.
> Cheap grace means justification of sin but not the sinner.
> Cheap grace is preaching forgiveness without repentance; it is baptism without the discipline of community; it is the Lord's Supper without confession of sin; it is absolution without personal confession. Cheap grace is grace without discipleship, grace without the cross, grace without the living, incarnate Jesus Christ.[89]

One of the key notions about cheap grace is that it is always offered as a presupposition rather than as a conclusion. In other words, it is predictable, mechanistic, and always available and at the disposal of the sinner. It is like a blank check or a bottomless bank account to which one has unlimited access to inexhaustible resources. Costly grace, by contrast, is never a presupposition—if it were, it would cease to be grace and would become necessary or even deserved—it can only be a conclusion. In other words, grace is always surprising, always transformative, always beyond what we can calculate or even imagine.[90] Furthermore, an invitation to costly grace is an invitation to join the kingdom of God, an invitation to become a disciple of the crucified, an invitation to live out the Sermon on the Mount; in short, it is an invitation to bear the cross daily. As Bonhoeffer poignantly puts it: "When Christ calls a man, he bids him come and die."[91]

A second problem with turning penal substitution into a methodology for evangelism is that it relies heavily on one particular type of experience, namely a deep sense of guilt and fear of divine punishment. One concern that Bonhoeffer raised about such an (over-)emphasis is that it quickly leads to manipulation. People are easily pushed into a "decision" for conversion when they are feeling feeble, destitute, and guilty. Bonhoeffer asks, "Are we to fall upon a few unfortunate people in their hour of

89. Bonhoeffer, *Discipleship*, 43–44.

90. Green and Baker worry that popular evangelical depictions of the cross have removed its scandal and enigma, and have turned it into a slogan (*Recovering the Scandal of the Cross*, 12).

91. Bonhoeffer, *The Cost of Discipleship*, 89.

need and exercise a sort of religious compulsion on them?"[92] It would not be difficult to show that our contemporary post-modern culture is highly skeptical of such ploys.

Another concern arises: What if people lack this sense of guilt and condemnation (which seems to be the case in contemporary Canada)? What if this particular experience of guilt is more prevalent in certain times, places, or cultures? Bonhoeffer recognized this problem and argued that the gospel must be contextualized and proclaimed to "good" and "happy" people, just as it is to "evil" and "despairing" people. He attacked the Lutheranism of his day because, in its fixation upon guilt, human weakness, and misery, it simply did not address "good" people.[93] Bonhoeffer laments, "But if [the 'good' person] cannot be brought to see and admit that his happiness is really an evil, his health sickness, and his vigour despair, the theologian is at his wit's end."[94] Bonhoeffer faults Lutheranism for narrowly directing the message of the gospel toward the "evil man" without considering how the "good man" might find Christ.[95] In Bonhoeffer's thinking, focusing on the former without the latter results in gospel reductionism, as the gospel becomes "merely the call to conversion and the consolation in sin of drunkards, adulterers and vicious men of every kind, and the gospel [loses] its power over good people."[96] In addition, by attending (almost exclusively) to human weakness and by downplaying human goodness, Bonhoeffer felt that Lutheranism unintentionally justified the lifestyles of those who lived self-indulgently and indifferently to the needs of others.

It is worth asking whether these same criticisms apply to our present-day North American evangelical churches, especially

92. Bonhoeffer, *Letters and Papers*, 280.

93. Bonhoeffer directs his criticism not at Luther *per se*, but at the Lutheran tradition that followed him, particularly in its nineteenth- and twentieth-century forms.

94. Bonhoeffer, *Letters and Papers*, 341.

95. Bonhoeffer, *Ethics*, 63.

96. Bonhoeffer, *Ethics*, 63–44.

with reference to our evangelistic and church growth strategies.[97] Do we turn penal substitution into a methodology? Do we favor one type of conversion experience over others? Do we ignore key aspect of the good news of the kingdom in our "gospel messages" in order to win converts?

5. *Conclusion*

The penal substitution view, when articulated by its best proponents, is a faithful interpretation of the atonement and continues to have significance for contemporary people. However, an appropriate contextualization of penal substitution in contemporary culture requires great care and discernment. In particular, it is crucial that we avoid the common errors of turning the metaphor into a metanarrative or a methodology. To avoid these pitfalls, it is best to adopt a multi-dimensional view of the atonement, which recognizes the significance of all of the atonement metaphors and attempts to speak into the complexity of the human condition.

97. McKnight argues that popular atonement theologies in North America have had a homogenizing effect and have been counter-productive to the gospel mandate of reconciliation (*Community Called Atonement*, 5).

Bibliography

Asselt, Willem J. van. "Christ's Atonement: A Multi-Dimensional Approach." *CTJ* 30 (2003) 52–67.

Boersma, Hans. "Eschatological Justice and the Cross: Violence and Penal Substitution." *ThTo* 60 (2003) 186–99.

———. "Penal Substitution and the Possibility of Unconditional Hospitality." *SJT* 57 (2004) 80–94.

Bonhoeffer, Dietrich. *The Cost of Discipleship*. A Touchstone Book. New York: Simon and Schuster, 1995.

———. *Discipleship*. Vol. 4 *Dietrich Bonhoeffer Works*. Edited by Geffrey B. Kelly and John D. Godsey. Minneapolis: Fortress Press, 2001.

———. *Ethics*. A Touchstone Book. New York: Simon and Schuster, 1995.

———. *Letters and Papers from Prison*. Enlarged Edition. Edited by Eberhard Bethge. New York: Macmillan, 1972.

Brock, Rita Nakashima. *Journeys by Heart: A Christology of Erotic Power*. New York: Crossroad, 1988.

Crysdale, Cynthia S. W. *Embracing Travail: Retrieving the Cross Today*. New York: Continuum, 1999.

Erickson, Millard J. *Christian Theology*, Vol. 2. Grand Rapids: Baker, 1984.

Green, Joel B. "Kaleidoscopic View." In *The Nature of the Atonement: Four Views*, edited by James Beilby and Paul R. Eddy, 157–201. Downers Grove: InterVarsity Press, 2006.

Green, Joel B. and Mark D. Baker. *Recovering the Scandal of the Cross: Atonement in New Testament and Contemporary Contexts*. Downers Grove: InterVarsity Press, 2000.

Grudem, Wayne. *Systematic Theology: An Introduction to Biblical Doctrine*. Leicester: Inter-Varsity Press/Grand Rapids: Zondervan, 1994.

Gunton, Colin E. *The Actuality of Atonement: A Study of Metaphor, Rationality and the Christian Tradition*. London: T. & T. Clark, 1988.

Hodge, Charles. *Systematic Theology*, Vol. 2. Peabody: Hendrickson, 1999.

Marshall, I. Howard. "The Death of Jesus in Recent New Testament Study." *WW* 3 (1983) 12–21.

McKnight, Scot. *A Community Called Atonement*. Nashville: Abingdon Press, 2007.

Morris, Leon. *The Apostolic Preaching of the Cross*. London: Tyndale Press, 1955.

———. *The Cross in the New Testament*. Grand Rapids: Eerdmans, 1965.

———. *The Cross of Jesus*. Grand Rapids: Eerdmans, 1988.

Ngien, Dennis. *The Suffering of God according to Martin Luther's* Theologia Crucis. Eugene, OR: Wipf and Stock, 1995.

Peterson, James C. *Genetic Turning Points: The Ethics of Human Genetic Intervention*. Grand Rapids: Eerdmans, 2001.

Schmiechen, Peter. *Saving Power: Theories of Atonement and Forms of the Church*. Grand Rapids/Cambridge: Eerdmans, 2005.

Weaver, Denny J. "The Violence of Satisfaction and the Satisfaction of Violence." *Mennonite Life* 59 Accessed March 30, 2009. Online: http://www.bethelks.edu/mennonitelife/2004June/weaver.php.

Wells, Paul. "A Free Lunch at the End of the Universe? Sacrifice, Substitution and Penal Liability." *Them* 29 (2003) 38–51.

[*MJTM* 10 (2008–2009) 53–68]

Contemporary Images for Communicating the Atonement and Redemption: Liberator and Lover

Andrew K. Gabriel
McMaster Divinity College, Hamilton, ON

Not all biblical and historical images of the atonement and redemption will communicate effectively in contemporary society. "Redemption," for example, generally connotes presenting a coupon for something; that is, one gives something that was received for free and gets a free benefit for it—a discount or a free item. This conflicts with the biblical idea of redemption as "a process involving release by payment of a ransom price."[1] Similarly, the terms "propitiation" or "expiation" (from the Greek *hilasmos*), found in older English Bible translations, today would be foreign words to most people, whether Christians or not. Other images would be more effective to communicate the meaning of the atonement today.

This paper will present two images of the atonement and redemption—God as Liberator and as Lover.[2] Both images will be described by considering what "the problem" (i.e., sin) is according to the images as proposed here, the action God takes, and the results of this action. These descriptions are not meant to exhaust the meaning and significance of the atonement, but are given to describe how each *particular* image can and does communicate the significance of the atonement. Two images of the atonement are presented primarily to reinforce the fact that every image (biblical or not) does not communicate all that is significant with respect to the atonement, but also to

1. Morris, *The Apostolic Preaching of the Cross*, 10.

2. Rick Warren also speaks of God as both Liberator and Lover, though he does not explicate his understanding of these images. See his influential book, *The Purpose Driven Life*, 79.

communicate more of the essential aspects of the atonement than if only one image was presented. By doing this I hope to avoid the "great loss" that occurs when "atonement theology . . . is collapsed into one model or metaphor."[3] Furthermore, it will become clear that in presenting these images I do not dismiss key historical expressions of the atonement (e.g., Christus victor, the satisfaction theory, or the moral influence theory), but rather draw on their strengths and seek to improve upon their weaknesses.

1. *Liberator*

The first image of the atonement to be explored presents God as the Liberator of humankind and the world. This will bear resemblance to the Christus victor model of the atonement, in which Christ is presented triumphant over the evil powers of the world, and may conjure ideas of liberation theology, but it will be seen that this presentation of God as Liberator is distinct from both. The image of Liberator is one that should have some impression upon a culture that is certainly familiar with the idea of liberation. Freedom is something we value and strive for. For example, we see commercials for retirement planning aiming at financial freedom, which exemplifies our desire for freedom from those things that restrain us. Similarly, the need for liberation is manifested in the self-help groups that abound.

The concept of God as Liberator is consistent with the biblical theme that God is the one who freed the people of Israel from slavery in Egypt. It is also consistent with Paul's assertion that we are "set free from sin" (Rom 6:18, 22; cf. 8:2). God is the Liberator who sets us free from sin that we might live in freedom. As expressed here, the metaphor of God as Liberator serves as an expression of atonement and redemption by presenting humanity as enslaved to sin and its effects, and God as the one who sets us free from this enslavement. I begin by discussing how humanity (and even creation at large) is enslaved to sin, and

3. Green and Baker, *Recovering the Scandal of the Cross*, 108.

then continue by discussing how the liberating work of God in the atonement remedies this situation.

A. *Enslavement*

According to this image, the problem with humanity and the world at large is that it is enslaved to sin and the results of sin. We are, in fact, even slaves to ourselves. As Cynthia Crysdale describes it, we are involved in self-destruction. Sin is more than "disobedience to a divine command but an innate conflict between who we are and who we can become."[4] With our very own choices we destroy ourselves. People are often unaware or uncertain of what is right. And even when we do know what is right, there is an inner conflict that rages on inside of us between us and us. As Paul wrote: "I know that nothing good lives in me, that is, in my sinful nature. For I have the desire to do what is good, but I cannot carry it out. For what I do is not the good I want to do; no, the evil I do not want to do—this I keep on doing" (Rom 7:18–19). This is because sin is not only an external thing, or actions that we do, but sin affects us deeply. It can even be described as "sin living in me" (Rom 7:20). As this sin lives in us, we are slaves to ourselves.

Our separation from God comes from this sin, which is self-serving and self-focused rather than God-serving. We become consumed with gaining things for ourselves and making a great name for ourselves rather than with worshipping God. Emil Brunner described sin like this: "Sin is the desire for the autonomy of man; therefore, in the last resort, it is the denial of God and self-deification: it is getting rid of the Lord God, and the proclamation of self-sovereignty."[5]

This obsession with ourselves not only causes us to destroy ourselves, but it may also destroy others. In an effort to save money by making things cheaply or in an effort to hoard money for ourselves, we rob others, oppress others, and treat others (both at home and globally) in ways that we would not allow

4. Crysdale, *Embracing Travail: Retrieving the Cross Today*, 9.

5. Brunner, *The Christian Doctrine of Creation and Redemption*, 92–93.

ourselves to be treated. Our own enslavement to sin causes us to enslave others with our political and economic acts.

We are also slaves to sin in that we are deceived. We have believed the lie that God does not love us. This shows that we do not know God. Ironically, at other times, we are deceived in that we "pervert the grace of our God into a license for immorality" (Jude 1:4). By doing this, we have often even deceived ourselves by convincing ourselves that sin is "not that bad." Overall, our own sin has caused us to enslave our minds. As a result, we are among those who have "exchanged the truth about God for a lie" (Rom 1:25). This is cognitive slavery to sin.

From a wider perspective, the creation at large is enslaved as a result of sin. It is "subjected to frustration" and itself needs to be "liberated from its bondage to decay" (Rom 8:20, 21). It would be fair to say that our manner of polluting the environment and destroying God's creation could be described as us making creation our slave.

From God's perspective, sin causes a problem in our relationship because he is holy. That is, he is without sin and he hates sin. God condemns us for our sin (cf. Rom 5:18) (we often do so ourselves). We, on the other hand, are enslaved to sin and can do nothing about it. This fact in and of itself is enslaving, for we recognize that, of ourselves, we are hopeless.

B. *Liberation*

In response to a world being enslaved by sin, God provides liberation. God, in his love, came as Jesus Christ and the Holy Spirit to set us free. This was done in spite of our enslavement—"while we were still sinners" (Rom 5:8). Christ came "that he might take away our sins" (1 John 3:5). As a result of this act of Christ, "he forgave us all our sins" (Col 2:13). Immediately we are set free from the torture of the recognition that we could not save ourselves—God has forgiven us; our hopelessness is removed.

In the forgiveness that results from the cross we are immediately free from much deception. We now recognize that God loves us. He was willing to do whatever it took in order to deal with our sin. We are also now free from the fear of God. As Peter Abelard wrote, "Christ's suffering . . . wins for us the true liberty of sons of God, so that we do all things out of love rather than fear."[6] Furthermore, we are free from the deception that sin is "not that bad." From the steps God took to free us from sin, we realize that this sin that enslaves us is in fact something serious and significant. Lastly, we are freed from the fear of death. We know that Christ was resurrected and, as the Spirit is now creating Christians into the image of Christ, we believe that we too will experience a resurrection similar to Christ's—there is life after death.

Even though we are forgiven from sin, in order for us to be free from condemnation for sin, we must be "in Christ." We have been offered the way to freedom, but we must accept it. That is, we must accept this forgiveness and be bound to Christ. It is only for those who are "in Christ" that "there is now no condemnation" (Rom 8:1). And yet, even though forgiven, being enslaved to sin, we are not able to accept this forgiveness. We must, in our present day, be freed from enslavement to sin before we can even turn to God in reception of this forgiveness. This is provided by the work of the Holy Spirit. He exposes the sin of the world (John 16:8) and draws us to Christ. He frees us from the deception that we are all that matters. He frees us from our self-worship and self-centered goals, allowing us to confess that "Jesus is Lord" (1 Cor 12:3).

Beyond the act of turning to God, the Holy Spirit works to guide us in our inner conflict with our sinful desires. Though we fail, he sets us free as he helps us grow in holiness. He produces fruit in us (Gal 5:22), leading us to the freedom of being able to live the righteous life that God desires. Paul expresses this idea throughout Romans chapter eight when he speaks of "the Spirit who gives life [and] has set you free from the law of sin and death" (8:2). In this chapter, Paul describes how "those who live according to the sinful nature have their minds set on what that nature desires; but those who live in accordance with the Spirit

6. Abelard, "Peter Abailard: Exposition of the Epistle to the Romans," 284.

have their minds set on what the Spirit desires. The mind controlled by the sinful nature is death, but the mind controlled by the Spirit is life and peace" (8:5–6). It is the Holy Spirit who frees people from the desires of sin so that they can experience this "life and peace."

As individuals are liberated from their enslavement to sin, God is likewise freeing others from enslavement to sin, and creation as a whole is being set free from its enslavement. Each person's sin affects others, and by setting us free from our individual ways of sin, the Holy Spirit is likewise liberating those whom we have enslaved by our sin—in our change to holy living we are no longer oppressing the world around us. Let us now turn to evaluate the image of God as Liberator.

C. *Evaluation*

The image of God as Liberator conveys a number of important aspects of the atonement. First, as with the Christus victor model, there is here a clear emphasis on the positive aspect of what has occurred. Where the penal substitution image of the atonement focuses on the removal and fulfillment of (negative) punishment, the image of God as Liberator focuses on the positive reception of freedom.

Second, there is a balance between the individual and communal (even cosmic) aspects of salvation. By contrast, in the satisfaction image, as presented by Anselm in *Cur Deus Homo*, each individual owes God a debt that is paid for in Christ's death. Likewise, in the moral influence concept of atonement, it is incumbent upon the individual to respond to God's revelation of love. Here, each person is pictured as enslaved to sin, but there is a realization that we are all enslaved together and that each person's enslavement affects the community around them. This extends beyond humanity to the cosmic community as well. That is, as humanity is redeemed from their slavery to sin, the effects of human sin upon creation at large are mitigated. This is an aspect of the atonement that is not generally included in the classical metaphors for the atonement.

Third, this image recognizes that the atonement is not limited to the cross, but includes all of salvation. As Gustaf Aulén recognized, the "Spirit ever triumphantly continues to break down sin's power."[7] Even though, by the cross, we are freed from some aspects of sin, there is a process of being freed from sin, of being made holy. We are still being freed from the effects of our enslavement even when we become Christians—the wounds of sin must be healed. Though this image has included discussion of the after-affects of Christ's death, it has remained an image of the atonement in that even though God has reconciled us to himself through Christ, we must still turn to God and be freed from sin before the relationship is finally reconciled completely. Only then are humans and God finally "at one."

Fourth, this image is helpful in that it does not present a violent image that might not be appreciated today. There is no presentation of God punishing Jesus, of which the penal substitution model is often accused, nor of a violent victory, as often presented in the Christus victor motif.[8]

Fifth, this image of God as Liberator emphasizes that the work of atonement is the work of God. It is only he who could set us free as we were utterly enslaved to our own sin. This is in contrast to the moral influence theory, which seems to suggest that the cross of Christ did not objectively accomplish anything, but that it only motivates us to respond. In the image of God as Liberator, there is recognition that (due to our sin) we need more than motivation to get out of our slavery to sin; we need someone to set us free.

Lastly, this image of God as Liberator is focused on God's relationship with humanity. It is about setting us free. This is in contrast to the Christus victor model which focuses on Christ's encounter with evil powers, rather than Christ's encounter with us. That is, the emphasis here is upon Christ *for us*, rather than *against them*.

7. Aulén, *Christus Victor*, 60.

8. E.g. Aulén, *Christus Victor*, 119, notes that "Luther loves violent expressions, strong colours, realistic images, and in innumerable passages, he describes Christ's conflict with the tyrants in this way."

We have noted numerous positive aspects of the above image of God as Liberator, but we must also consider a possible drawback of this image. The image of God as Liberator might seem to be lacking, in that it might appear to mislead people. That is, just as we are liberated by God, we also become slaves of Christ (as Paul often reminds us). This truth does not contradict this image, however, because being a slave for Christ sets us free to be what we were truly made to be and to live the life we were meant to live. Accordingly, John Stott notes, "God's love in Christ, which has in one sense liberated us, in another hems us in, because it leaves us no alternative but to live the rest of our lives for him, in adoring and grateful service."[9] Becoming a slave of Christ does not indicate oppression, but rather a choice of "grateful service."

2. *Lover*

The second image of the atonement to be proposed here is that of God as our faithful Lover (or Spouse). The image of "Lover" finds a basis as Paul discusses the husband-wife relationship and then concludes by adding, "This is a profound mystery—but I am talking about Christ and the church" (Eph 5:32). This image is also based upon the biblical concept of "reconciliation." It should have an impression upon our culture in which broken relationships are not uncommon. In particular, for those who choose to commit to marriage, the relationship often ends in divorce. In addition, employing the idea of reconciliation is attractive in that it is the opposite of alienation, which many people feel today. Stott suggests that people often "do not feel at home in the materialism, emptiness and superficiality of the western world. On the contrary, they feel unfulfilled and disoriented, unable to find themselves, their identity or their freedom."[10] This image presents God as the faithful Lover[11] who

9. Stott, *The Cross of Christ*, 257.
10. Stott, *The Cross of Christ*, 193.

seeks to restore his relationship with his adulterous beloved, his human creatures. I begin by describing how humanity has been "adulterous" in their relationship with God along with the shame that results from this. I then continue by describing how God continues loving us in spite of this, and seeks to reconcile us to him, even to the point of taking on the shame of the adulterer through the atonement.

A. *Adultery*

The emphasis in this image is that God's creation (here speaking only of humanity), which he loves, has been unfaithful in its relationship with God. God created us out of love and he wanted to have a loving relationship with us. We, however, have been adulterous, not loving God by not obeying him (John 14:15; 1 John 5:3). We have turned from him and committed adultery by "sleeping" with another. Jeremiah speaks of Israel's sins as having "committed adultery with stone and wood" (Jer 3:9; cf. Ezek 23:37). Rather than loving God and staying faithful we turn to the ways of the world. We have loved the world and ourselves and have forsaken God. In this manner, we read "You adulterous people, don't you know that friendship with the world is hatred toward God?" (Jas 4:4).

From our adultery, we experience shame. As a result of shame we feel worthless, and (correctly) unworthy to return to our Lover, God. C. Norman Kraus describes shame: "uncleanliness, weakness, or blemish and its consequences devaluate the worth and self-esteem of the sinner."[12] In our shame we feel we do not deserve to be accepted. Our shame and our fear that God may reject us inhibit us from returning to God. Instead, rather than trying to return to our Lover, we remain in our adultery, hoping to find acceptance elsewhere and fulfillment in this sin.

11. The inclusion of "faithful" is important because the term "Lover" alone might also be found in the context of one who is unfaithful and acting adulterously.

12. Kraus, *Jesus Christ Our Lord*, 212.

B. *Reconciliation*

The Lover is angry about our adultery. It grieves God. Nevertheless, the Lover does not stop loving us. If he did not love us, he would not have cared about our adultery. And so, this love that creates anguish within God is the same love that causes God, the Lover, to seek reconciliation with us.[13] God's love must be satisfied![14] God loves us despite our adultery. Accordingly, the Lord said to Hosea, "Go, show your love to your wife again, though she is loved by another and is an adulteress. Love her as the Lord loves the Israelites, though they turn to other gods and love the sacred raisin cakes" (Hos 3:1).[15]

Because of his love, God came to us. He came after us to tell us he loves us. He came to reconcile us to himself. He came as a human—Jesus Christ. Though we did not turn to God for forgiveness, and though we do not deserve to remain in relationship with God, "God was reconciling the world to himself in Christ," and rather than chastising us for our adultery, he was "not counting people's sins against them" (2 Cor 5:19, TNIV).

Though we deserved shame, and were shamed, God came and took our shame upon himself. Joel B. Green and Mark D. Baker note:

> Although we tend to emphasize the physical pain of death on the cross, in the Roman era crucifixion was dreaded first and foremost because of its shameful character. It was designed to be an instrument of contempt and public ridicule. The victim died naked, in bloody sweat, helpless to control body excretions. . . . By Roman law no

13. Cf. Calvin, *Institutes*, II.16.4: "Accordingly in a manner wondrous and divine, he loved even when he hated us."

14. Cf. Stott, *The Cross of Christ*, 129, who writes, "It is not even only that he must satisfy his law, his honour, his justice, or the moral order: it is that he must satisfy *himself* . . . [The concept of God's holy love] insists on the satisfaction of God himself in *every* aspect of his being, including both his justice and his *love*" (my emphasis [Stott's emphasis on "every"]).

15. Granted, there are times when the biblical images of marriage and adultery appear *not* to end in reconciliation between God and his people. E.g., "I gave faithless Israel her certificate of divorce and sent her away because of all her adulteries" (Jer 3:8).

> citizen could be disgraced through this dishonorable means of execution.[16]

In taking our shame, the Lover showed that he was willing to identify with us even in our shame. But rather than allowing us and others to focus on our shortcomings, causing our shame to continue, he took the shame for us. In "the substitution of total identification which accepts responsibility" for us, "he took our place including the consequences of this identification."[17] He became sin for us (2 Cor 5:21). Our shame is no longer recognized. Furthermore, where God has identified with us in our shameful state, we are invited to now identify with him outside of shame in a place of reconciliation with him. In terms of Christ's work, Kraus notes, Jesus Christ's "identification with us in our shameful situation enables us to identify with him in his realization of 'the glorious liberty of the children of God' (Rom 8:21)."[18] As a result, those who trust in him "will never be put to shame" (1 Pet 2:6), for they have been reconciled to their Lover.

Furthermore, in taking on our shame, God has shown us how much he loves us. In coming to us and taking the shame that was ours upon himself, he draws us to him. He has shown us how much he loves us and wants us back. As a result, "we love because he first loved us" (1 John 4:19). From God's act of reconciliation, we realize how much God loves us. We are also no longer afraid of him. We know that he wants us back and that he will accept us. This causes our hearts to soften. We are able to come out of our experience of shame and be reconciled to God.

As with the image of God as Liberator, God the Lover, having reconciled us through Christ, still reconciles us to himself today. Accordingly, even after the death of Christ, Paul was able to admonish the Corinthians, "Be reconciled to God" (2 Cor 5:20). God continues wooing us back to himself by means of the Holy Spirit. He reminds us of the truth of what God, in Christ, has done for us (John 14:26; 16:13).

16. Green and Baker, *Recovering the Scandal of the Cross*, 163.
17. Kraus, *Jesus Christ Our Lord*, 219.
18. Kraus, *Jesus Christ Our Lord*, 218.

C. *Evaluation*

The image of God as faithful Lover who reconciles his adulterous beloved communicates a number of important aspects of the atonement. In all of the historical images of the atonement one finds that sin is a problem that somehow affects our relationship with God. Accordingly, Aulén writes, "The essential character of salvation is a reconciliation, the re-establishment of a broken fellowship between God and the world."[19] This image focuses in on this reality. This is its first advantage: it presents the atonement as something personal between God and humanity. By contrast, Hans Boersma notes that "Traditional Protestant readings of St Paul . . . work with a strict economy of exchange: the covenantal relationship between God and human beings takes on strongly contractual connotations."[20] The image of God as Lover shows, in a relational way, why God came to humanity in the incarnation—he was coming to where we were, in order to reconcile us back to him.

A second advantage of this image is that it emphasizes God's love. By contrast, note Aulén's comments regarding the Lutheran tradition:

> The idea of God which underlies it is, above all, that of a Justice which imposes its law and demands satisfaction. Only within these limits is the Divine Love allowed to operate, and there is a suggestion that the idea of the *Divine Love is regarded with some suspicion*, as though it needed to be watched lest it should infringe on the demands of justice.[21]

In contrast, the image of God as Lover emphasizes that it is not only God's justice that must be satisfied in the atonement, but God's love must also be satisfied. That is, the love of God that has been grieved by the break in the relationship by the adulterer seeks to restore this broken relationship. In this way, God's love is satisfied.

19. Aulén, *Christus Victor*, 225.
20. Boersma, "Penal Substitution," 92.
21. Aulén, *Christus Victor*, 146 (my emphasis).

Third, as with the image of God as Liberator, this image does not create a rift in God. God (Father, Son, and Holy Spirit) is seen throughout the whole image as the Lover who is pursuing reconciliation with his beloved. In contrast, especially when interpreting the penal substitution theory, it can appear (wrongly) as though the (mean) Father is a bloodthirsty God who requires that someone be punished (anyone!) because of sin and that the (nice) Jesus Christ comes to "save the day," by saving us from the Father. Such a misinterpretation of the atonement is not likely to happen with the image of God as the divine Lover.

Fourth, presenting the problem of sin as creating a problem of shame has unique advantages. It implies that this image of the atonement recognizes that feelings other than guilt might accompany sin. That is, this image appeals to the feeling of shame rather than just a sense of deserved punishment. In addition, viewing sin as shame presents sin as something internal to us that must be reckoned with, rather than just something external (e.g., death and the devil) that must be defeated, as in the Christus victor model. In other words, we are part (a large part) of the problem that calls for the need of the atonement and redemption.

A few more brief comments may be made regarding the positive aspects of the atonement that the image of God as Lover communicates. As with the image of God as Liberator, the image of God as Lover recognizes that atonement—reconciliation—is not limited to the cross, but includes all of salvation. Moreover, this image has also emphasized that God is the one who has initiated the act of reconciliation—humans are not able to save themselves. And, lastly, this image presents a non-violent notion of the atonement.

Several weaknesses and limitations of the image of God as Lover may also be noted. Nevertheless, most of these weaknesses are balanced (i.e., corrected) when the image is presented together with the image of God as Liberator. First, this image is individualistic—the Lover seeks his beloved. However, though Christ died for individuals, he died for all people—"He is the atoning sacrifice for our sins, and not only for ours but also for the sins of the whole world" (1 John 2:2). Similarly, this image of atonement focuses only on the God-human relationship. By contrast, it appears that by Christ's death on the cross "all things" have been reconciled to God (Col 1:20). In other words, this image of the atonement does not deal with the cosmic effects of the atonement as well as the image of God as Liberator does. However, this only serves to remind us that no model can by itself exhaust the meaning of the atonement.

This points to a second *possible* weakness of this image. The image of reconciliation presupposes that the relationship being reconciled is one that existed previously. In the context of this image we might ask, were we "married" before the adultery? Certainly, in the larger perspective of the biblical story of creation, fall, redemption, and consummation, the answer is "yes"; prior to the fall, humanity was "married" to God. However, when it comes to considering each individual person (post-fall), the answer will depend on one's doctrine of original sin. If one is born a guilty sinner who needs to be reconciled to God, then the individualistic aspect of this image does not fully communicate the idea of reconciliation. On the other hand, if an infant does not have "original guilt," then the image of Lover, which presents the idea of reconciliation on an individual level, is presenting some truth regarding an individual's relationship with God in the sense that initially they were not alienated from God.

Third, "God as Lover" does not communicate the propitiatory nature of the cross. That is, it does not adequately describe how Christ's death appeases God's wrath, nor has it recognized God's wrath (though it has recognized his anger). This might seem like a significant shortcoming to some people. However, many other accounts of the atonement miss how God's love is at the heart of why atonement is needed! This of course, is something that this image portrays quite well. Again, the various images of the atonement can complement one another in this area.

Conclusion

In light of the need for contemporary ways to describe the atonement and redemption, I have presented the images of God as Liberator and God as faithful Lover. Neither image is meant to be exhaustive; they are meant to complement each other. They also complement, and at times supplement, traditional concepts and terms that are used to communicate the atonement. However, in contrast to these traditional ways of communicating the atonement (some in the Bible itself and others throughout Christian history), which sometimes obscure the meaning of the atonement for contemporary people, the images of God as Liberator and faithful Lover present ideas that are meaningful for contemporary hearers. Especially in our current economic climate, people are familiar with the need to be liberated from the poor choices that people might make. The image of God as Liberator presents God as liberating people from poor sinful choices in particular. Similarly, the breakdown of relationships in contemporary society allows the image of God as faithful Lover to possess unique explanatory power for our culture when communicating the atonement.

I conclude with a quote from John Stott that may be comforting when our communication of the cross and the atonement seems inadequate: "For beyond the images of the atonement lies the mystery of the atonement, the deep wonders of which, I guess, we shall be exploring throughout eternity."[22]

Bibliography

Abelard, Peter. "Peter Abailard: Exposition of the Epistle to the Romans (An Excerpt from the Second Book)." In *A Scholastic Miscellany: Anselm to Ockham*, edited and translated by Eugene R. Fairweather, 276–87. Philadelphia: Westminster, 1956.

Aulén, Gustaf. *Christus Victor*. New York: MacMillan, 1969.

Boersma, Hans. "Penal Substitution and the Possibility of Unconditional Hospitality." *SJT* 57 (2004) 80–94.

22. Stott, *The Cross of Christ*, 168.

Brunner, Emil. *The Christian Doctrine of Creation and Redemption: Dogmatics*. Vol. 2. Translated by Olive Wyon. Philadelphia: Westminster Press, 1952.

Calvin, John. *Institutes of the Christian Religion*. Edited by John T. McNeill. Translated by Ford Lewis Battles. Philadelphia: Westminster, 1960.

Crysdale, Cynthia S. W. *Embracing Travail: Retrieving the Cross Today*. New York: Continuum, 2000.

Green, Joel B., and Mark D. Baker. *Recovering the Scandal of the Cross: Atonement in New Testament and Contemporary Contexts*. Downers Grove, IL: InterVarsity Press, 2000.

Kraus, C. Norman. *Jesus Christ Our Lord: Christology from a Disciple's Perspective*. Scottdale, PA: Herald Press, 1990.

Morris, Leon. *The Apostolic Preaching of the Cross*. 3rd ed. Grand Rapids: Eerdmans, 1965.

Stott, John. *The Cross of Christ*. Downers Grove, IL: InterVarsity Press, 1986.

Warren, Rick. *The Purpose Driven Life*. Grand Rapids: Zondervan, 2002.

[*MJTM* 10 (2008–2009) 69–74]

LOSING CHRISTIANITY: A NEW TESTAMENT SCHOLAR'S FALL FROM FAITH (A REVIEW ARTICLE)

Stephen J. Bedard
Meaford, ON

Bart D. Ehrman. *Misquoting Jesus: The Story behind Who Changed the Bible and Why*. New York: HarperCollins, 2005. iv + 266 pp. Pbk. US$14.95.

Bart D. Ehrman. *Lost Christianities: The Battles for Scripture and the Faiths We Never Knew*. New York: Oxford University Press, 2003. xv + 294 pp. Pbk. US$19.99.

Academic authors often struggle with getting other scholars to read their works. New Testament scholar Bart Ehrman has achieved something very significant in taking extremely academic subjects, such as textual criticism and varieties of early Christianity, and turning them into bestsellers that have captured the public's imagination. Although *Misquoting Jesus* and *Lost Christianities* are separate books dealing with different issues, there is a common thread in the purposes of the author and so they will be reviewed together.

I will review *Misquoting Jesus* first, although it is the more recent book, as it is in the introduction to this book that Ehrman makes explicit the belief system that is the foundation for all of his recent projects. In this introduction, Ehrman presents a passionate and moving account of his conversion, first of all to evangelical Christianity, and secondly to agnosticism. After becoming a Christian as a young man, Ehrman began his theological education, developing a high view of Scripture in such conservative schools as Moody and Wheaton. However, it was while doing his doctoral work at Princeton that Ehrman came to a crisis of faith. Encountering a difficulty in the Gospels that he was unable to resolve, Ehrman received the suggestion from his professor that perhaps Mark simply made a mistake. Ehrman accepted this explanation, then reasoned that if there was one mistake in the Bible, the trustworthiness of Scripture based upon the doctrine of inspiration crumbled in disarray. Ehrman has since become just as zealous for demonstrating the problems of traditional Christianity as he once was for defending its truth.

Misquoting Jesus is an examination and presentation of the issues concerning textual criticism. Ehrman is certainly qualified to speak on such matters, having studied under the late Bruce Metzger. Ehrman begins with a summary on the beginnings of Christian Scripture, including the emergence of Christianity from Judaism, the appearance of various genres in early Christian writings, and the development of the canon. Apart from any limitations that Ehrman might see in the original documents, it is the topic of the copying of the documents over the centuries that is the heart of this book. Ehrman provides a helpful study on the methods and issues surrounding copying, both in the Greco-Roman world and the early church, providing examples from the testimony of early Church Fathers. Not only can both accidental and intentional changes be demonstrated in many of the manuscripts of the New Testament, Ehrman also reveals the limitations of the printed Greek New Testaments as they began to appear in the sixteenth century. He provides a nice account of the various scholars who worked with the Greek texts in attempts to reconstruct the New Testament wording in a form as close to the original as possible.

The heart of *Misquoting Jesus* is the investigation of changes that have been made in the Greek texts by copyists throughout the ages. Although the majority of these changes were accidental, that is, common mistakes made by honest Christian scribes, Ehrman is particularly interested in the deliberate changes made as a result of theological and social agendas. Ehrman concludes by stating, "The more I studied the manuscript tradition of the New Testament, the more I realized just how radically the text had been altered over the years at the hands of scribes, who were not only conserving scripture but also changing it."[1] Ehrman implies that, because of these difficulties, our present New Testament is not a reliable representation of the original New Testament, much less an accurate account of the historical Jesus and the beliefs of the early church. All of this fits very closely with Ehrman's own loss of faith as described in the introduction.

Ehrman should be commended for making such an academic subject an interest for so many people in the public. Ehrman has a lively and engaging writing style that draws the reader in, even when describing ancient copying methods or Reformation attempts at reconstructing the Greek New Testament. Ehrman obviously has a very strong interest in the material and an excellent grasp of the issues that make *Misquoting Jesus* an important book.

Unfortunately there are problems with *Misquoting Jesus*. Ehrman is unable to detach his presentation of issues regarding textual criticism from his own abandonment of the faith. Each chapter seems to be designed as an apologetic for skeptics like himself who have chosen to leave the Christian faith. Ehrman presents texts such as John 7:53–8:11, Mark 16:9–20 and the long version of 1 John 5:7 almost as the church's attempt to pass forgeries as originals, even though most modern translations make it very clear that these were later additions. It would be wise us for us to remember the words of Ehrman's teacher Bruce Metzger who stated, "Lest the foregoing examples of alterations should give the impression that scribes were altogether willful and capricious in transmitting ancient copies of the New Testament, it ought to be noted that other evidence points to the careful and painstaking work on the part of many copyists."[2] Unlike Metzger, who remained confident of our ability to reconstruct the earliest and most reliable form of the text, Ehrman

1. Ehrman, *Misquoting Jesus*, 209. Note that Metzger only gave a page and a half to intentional changes in his classic treatment on textual criticism (Metzger, *Text of the New Testament*, 195–96).

2. Metzger, *Text of the New Testament*, 206.

presents a pessimistic picture of a hopelessly corrupt text.[3] While that may be one possible interpretation of the evidence, in other ways *Misquoting Jesus* is self-refuting. Throughout his book, Ehrman uses textual criticism to demonstrate what he believes to be the original form of the text. While he may be trying to shock readers with his interpretations, he is in fact demonstrating that text critical methods are sufficient to reconstruct the text. Ehrman never brings the fact that he makes these reconstructions to its logical conclusion: the fact that we have the quantity and quality of Greek texts to reconstruct the earliest New Testament texts with a high level of certainty.

Ehrman's *Lost Christianities* is written on a different subject, yet it also promotes his agenda of casting doubt on the trustworthiness of traditional Christianity. Ehrman begins with case studies of four representative examples of non-canonical books: the *Gospel of Peter*, the *Acts of Paul and Thecla*, the Coptic *Gospel of Thomas*, and the *Secret Gospel of Mark*. Ehrman organizes these texts under the clever categories of the ancient discovery of a forgery, the ancient forgery of a discovery, the discovery of an ancient forgery and the forgery of an ancient discovery. By looking at these four very different texts, Ehrman gives a good sample of the type of issues encountered when looking at non-canonical writings. In the second section, Ehrman looks at some of the movements in the early church that were responsible for some of the writings of interest including the Ebionites, Marcionites, Gnostics, and the group that would become the Orthodox. The third part shows Ehrman's real purpose for writing *Lost Christianities*, and that is to demonstrate the early diversity of Christianity and all that was "lost" when the proto-orthodox "stamped out" rival groups and enforced their own version of Christianity.

One of the strengths of *Lost Christianities* is the same as that of *Misquoting Jesus*, and that is: Ehrman is a talented writer and

3. Metzger concluded his work by stating that, despite a number of difficult passages, "in very many cases the textual critic is able to ascertain without residual doubt which reading must have stood as the original" (Metzger, *Text of the New Testament*, 246).

he is able to present academic subjects with wit and style. He draws the reader in and one can easily imagine the debates and feuds that took place within early Christianity. *Lost Christianities* is a good introduction to a sampling of non-canonical texts and an interesting but short summary of the movements that existed in the first few centuries of the Christian era.

The problem with *Lost Christianities* is the same as with *Misquoting Jesus*. Ehrman's agenda of trying to discredit traditional Christianity overwhelms his treatment of the subject. Ehrman agrees with the current popular idea that the church did not *begin* with the orthodox church from which numerous heresies broke off, but rather, diversity marked the church from the beginning with the orthodox church only gradually overcoming the others.[4] Of course there was diversity within the earliest church. One can find some variety of style and focus even within the books of the New Testament. However, there is not even a hint in our earliest texts of the radical theological diversity that we find among the Ebionites, Marcionites, Gnostics, and orthodox. Another problem is the claim that the orthodox form of Christianity was not the original form from which the other groups broke off. Even within our earliest texts, such as Paul's letters, we have claims of the divinity of Jesus, an idea that was foreign to the Ebionites. The entire New Testament has a heavy reliance on the Old Testament and has continuity with that redemptive history, but the Marcionites and Gnostics rejected the Old Testament background. There is a clear trajectory between the teachings of the New Testament and what became the orthodox Christian faith. Since the texts that support the other movements are from the late second century or after, it makes better sense to suggest that the proto-orthodox faith was original and the other movements were schisms from the original form of Christianity.

There is no doubt that Bart Ehrman is a major figure, not just in New Testament scholarship, but in public debates on religion. Ehrman is a talented writer who knows how to connect with his

4. For a helpful response to this idea see Bock, *The Missing Gospels: Unearthing the Truth behind Alternative Christianities*.

readers and how to present academic information that is both understandable and interesting. Unfortunately, both *Misquoting Jesus* and *Lost Christianities* are driven more by a desire for an apologetic for Ehrman's own de-conversion than a desire to present information. Ehrman has a strong agenda to try to discredit traditional Christianity, a task that these and subsequent books have attempted. Both books are worth reading, as much for what they say about current religious trends and debates as for information on the actual subjects.

Bibliography

Bock, Darrell L. *The Missing Gospels: Unearthing the Truth behind Alternative Christianities*. Nashville: Thomas Nelson, 2006.

Metzger, Bruce M. *The Text of the New Testament: Its Transmission, Corruption and Restoration*. New York: Oxford University Press, 1968.

[*MJTM* 10 (2008–2009) 75–100]

PREACHING SUBVERSIVELY: THE BOOK OF ESTHER AS A HOMILETICAL MODEL

Lee Beach
McMaster Divinity College, Hamilton, ON

Introduction

Samuel Beckett's play *Waiting for Godot* is famous for the nonappearance of the play's primary character. The play unfolds as two friends, Estragon and Vladimir, pass the time waiting for the appearance of the illusive Godot. While Godot is central to the play and his anticipated introduction to the action drives the unfolding plot, he never appears on stage. In biblical literature, the book of Esther speaks of God's people in exile and the dramatic events that threaten their very existence and delineate their deliverance. Yet God is never mentioned. While it can be argued that God is the central character of the book and the driving force behind the unfolding plot, just like Godot in Beckett's play, he never makes an appearance in the story.

If a play can be driven by a character that never appears, and a biblical book can be canonized without ever mentioning God, can we preach a sermon about God without actually mentioning the word (or name) "God"? Asked in the context of homiletics, this is a provocative question. Are there any models, outside of narrative theory, that may suggest a positive response to this question? Certainly the aforementioned Old Testament book of Esther is a candidate for such a model.

This article will examine the story of Esther and seek to accomplish two things: first, to analyze how Esther functions as a narrative designed to encourage and instruct Israel during their exile; second, to examine how such a narrative approach could be suggestive as a contemporary homiletical method. It is well known that the book of Esther does not mention the divine name. Thus, the focus of this article is on the question, *how can a sermon speak about God without ever mentioning God?* It is undeniable that Esther functions as Holy Scripture without explicit mention of God in its pages. Perhaps, in a similar way, Esther provides an example of how a narrative sermon can speak powerfully about God without ever mentioning his name.

1. *Narrative as a Theological and Homiletical Tool*

Before proceeding with the question at hand, perhaps a brief review of the Esther story would be helpful. Esther is an orphaned Jewish girl raised by her cousin Mordecai. Esther is identified early as a beautiful young woman, and when the king of Persia is looking for a new wife, Esther ends up in the beauty contest whose winner will be named queen. As the contest transpires, Esther is the contestant who most pleases the king with her beauty and various other charms and is thus crowned the new queen of Persia. Throughout the process, at the urging of Mordecai, she conceals her Jewish identity. Shortly after her appointment as queen, a royal official named Haman talks the king into issuing an edict that will have the entire Jewish population of Persia exterminated. Hearing of the plot, Mordecai urges Esther to use her influence as queen to intervene on behalf of her people. Despite great personal risk, and through a series of remarkable coincidences and plot reversals, Esther manages to demonstrate to the king that Haman is a man of questionable character, and she is able to secure deliverance for her people. Her cousin Mordecai is elevated to be vice-regent of Persia and many Persian people convert to Judaism as a result of Esther's actions.

Esther, set as it is in Judah's exile,[1] was, or came to be understood as, a story that informed the exilic experience of

1. Technically the Persian period is usually known as the "post-exilic" period. While this term is traditionally used in Old Testament scholarship there is a clear sense in which Jews living under Persian rule were still exiled in that they did not have political autonomy even in their own land. For those who

Israel. It became a story that somehow depicted the lived experience of a diasporic people and created the potential for them to see their lives through the lens of an orphan girl who became a queen.

Over time, this book found its way into the Hebrew canon because it was deemed to be a "sacred story," not because it talked about God, but because it helped a nation understand its own story.[2] Narratives can function in this way in the life of a community, shaping its theological identity and guiding its behavior, even when they are not overtly theological.

This is the constitutive power of narrative. A story can reshape and define the world for us as we see ourselves in the characters, and sense our understanding of the world being described or reframed. Educators throughout history have understood the power of stories to both equip students with knowledge that they will need for later, and shape them into the kind of human beings we hope that they will become.[3]

Sermons are foundational avenues for shaping the theological and ethical life of a church. Thus, narrative forms of sermons can provide a lens through which people can see themselves, and offer possibilities for construing their lives both within the faith community and outside of it. By telling a congregation stories, a preacher can form the collective life of the church and the individual lives that compose it. Author Robert Fulford reflects on the power of story and reminds us that "Children grow into adults by learning stories, and so do nations and communities."[4]

Employing narrative as a form of preaching is not a new idea. It is at the heart of the "new homiletic" and has been well championed by many contemporary preachers. Stanley Hauwerwas states, "My contention is that the narrative mode is neither incidental nor accidental to Christian belief. There is no more

remained outside the land, like the characters in Esther, exile may still be an apt description of the life setting.

2. For insight on the concept of sacred story, see Crites, "The Narrative Quality of Experience," 70.

3. Jackson, "On the Place of Narrative in Teaching," 4.

4. Fulford, *Triumph of Narrative*, 33.

fundamental way to talk of God than in a story."[5] Thus, human stories explain, extend, and contextualize the story of God in fresh, new ways. The question under consideration in this study is whether this can be done in any meaningful sense without mentioning God in the story. To examine this question let us turn our attention to the Bible and the book of Esther.

2. *Esther: A Theological Narrative without Divine Reference*

a. *Esther as Exilic Literature*

The book of Esther is clearly set in the Persian period, when King Ahasuerus (Xerxes I) was ruler (486–465 BCE). The majority of scholars agree that a precise date for the book is hard to determine.[6] It is generally assumed, however, that the final Hebrew form of Esther is of late Persian or early Hellenistic origin.[7] From a purely literary perspective it seems obvious that the Esther scroll, which is foundational to the Jewish celebration of Purim, was written to demonstrate the potential of exilic life for those still trapped in such an existence.[8] While the writer never explicitly states the purpose for writing, the predominant theories all surround the idea that the writer desires to communicate something about life in exile.

For the community to thrive in exile, it would take more than just going back to former practices. A fresh interpretation of faith would be necessary, not only to sustain it but to meet the challenges of a new life setting. Walter Brueggemann articulates

5. Stanley Hauerwas, *The Peaceable Kingdom.* Notre Dame: Notre Dame University Press, 1983, 24–25, as cited in Jackson, "On the Place of Narrative in Teaching," 9.

6. For a concise but thorough discussion see Fox, *Character and Ideology*, 39–41.

7. Ibid. Also see also, Bechtel, *Esther*, 3. Bechtel reflects the breadth of opinion as well as the "agreement" among scholars that Esther is to be dated somewhere between 400 and 200 BCE.

8. This said, Berg, *Book of Esther*, 15, points out the difficulty of determining an author's intention when it is not explicitly stated, as is the case with the author of Esther.

how exile prompted the people of Israel to respond with creative expressions of theological thought:

> Exile did not lead Jews in the Old Testament to abandon faith or to settle for abdicating despair, nor to retreat to privatistic religion. On the contrary, exile evoked the most brilliant literature and the most daring theological articulation in the Old Testament.[9]

This was a theological imperative for the people of Israel now seeking to understand themselves and their God in fresh ways as a result of the new circumstances of exilic life. One of the ways the community found to express its theology of exile was through narratives designed to embody, in the characters, a diasporic lifestyle that demonstrated wisdom for exilic living. These "advice tales" feature heroes and heroines who offer a "lived out" theology of exile. These stories are theological novellas, whose purpose is to creatively engender in the people of Israel a vision for how to live successfully as a displaced people.

b. *Esther as a "Diasporic Advice Story"*

In the days of diasporic existence, narratives concerning the lives of exiles were a common form of didactic literature. These narratives depict Jewish men or women living in exilic situations who are able to thrive in their displaced context and even rise to significant places of influence. These characters appear in diasporic novellas that illustrate how these clever, pious heroes overcome much more powerful members of the dominant ethnic group and gain favor from the king.[10] These diasporic advice stories are presented throughout Scripture and stand as wisdom stories for the Israelite community to draw upon for diasporic living.

These tales, many of which probably emanate from the post-exilic period, inform the lives of a people whose land and fate is not fully their own. They include the stories of Esther, Mordecai,

9. Bruggemann, *Cadences of Home*, 3.
10. Smith, *Religion of the Landless*, 203.

Daniel, Joseph, Jonah, and Ruth.[11] Daniel Smith-Christopher offers that these stories are designed to reflect the Jews' rise to power and influence in the world, not through the use of reason or human ability, but through their excellence of character and faith in God.[12]

Such stories are typical of displaced peoples. It is often the narratives of a people that most vividly depict their understanding of life as it really is and express their beliefs about the best way forward. Roger Bromley, in his work on contemporary diasporic cultural fictions, notes that the stories of displaced peoples

> can be seen as participating in new cultural strategies . . . The essence of this work is the cultural analysis to go beyond the boundaries and exceed the limits of racialised, colonized and national identities. They are not simply narratives about contestation and difference, but achieve their very textualisation through constructions of difference and contestation.[13]

The authors of Scripture understood this power of narrative for forming a people's theology and vision for life in exile. The book of Esther clearly reflects characteristics that make it an advice tale for exiled Israel.

c. *Esther as Advice to a Diasporic People*

Many competing theories that have been offered to capture the exact genre of Esther.[14] Each one, however, acknowledges that there is a didactic nature to the book and most agree that it has a theological agenda as well.[15] In the current study I will adopt the

11. Variations of these stories can be seen in Ezra and Nehemiah. Jonah, while quite different, may also be viewed as a diasporic advice story, as it deals with God's interaction with foreign peoples and informs the post-exilic community as they seek to develop a theology of engagement with a wicked enemy nation. See Smith-Christopher, *Biblical Theology of Exile*, 130–37.

12. Ibid., 185.

13. Bromley, *Narratives for a New Belonging*, 3.

14. See Fox, *Character and Ideology*, 141–52.

15. See, for example, the influential work of Humphries, "A Life-style for Diaspora," 214. Humphries points out the delightfully entertaining nature of the Esther tale and acknowledges that this alone may "be reason enough" for its

position that Esther is a "Diaspora Advice Story." This label can encompass several of the potential genres often proposed to capture the essence of the scroll (such as "diaspora novella," "wisdom tale," and even "historical fiction"). Its diasporic nature is obvious; the term "advice story" is accurate because it rises above simply being a "good story." While it is indeed a fast-paced and suspenseful tale, its didactic purposes cannot be ignored. It is meant to teach Jews how to live a productive life in the Diaspora.[16]

Both Esther and Mordecai become characters in an "applied" theological narrative demonstrating to subsequent generations of Jews (and others) how the wisdom of God, through his prophetic word, informs life for a minority people in a culture governed by powers and laws different from and even contradictory to their own. Donn Morgan points out that while these writings may not be a direct response to the Torah and the Prophets, they do depict a dialogue between the interpretive communities and these writings.[17] Rooted in this dialogue/response to the Law and Prophets. Morgan sees that:

> The behavior of the characters provides paradigmatic actions and situations, which the reader or hearer is to ponder. The success of this behavior may provide an impetus for similar behavior in analogous situations or may simply testify to the value of faithfulness and allegiance to God and Judaism.[18]

d. *Dilemma: Where is God in Esther?*

Esther is well known as the only book in the Bible that does not mention the name of God. This omission has brought about more

existence. However, he goes on to demonstrate that the author has much more in mind than just this. See also Bechtel, *Esther*, 4.

16. White, "Esther a Feminine Model," 164. White also notes, "This sort of tale enjoyed great popularity in the post-exilic period" (164). For further reflection of scholarly consensus on this issue, see Talmon, "Wisdom in the Book of Esther." He states, "The point of the narrative is to portray 'applied' wisdom, that is, how a wise man [*sic*] may lead a successful life in the world" (441).

17. Morgan, *Between Text and Community*, 51.

18. Ibid., 52.

than its share of speculation. Some modern scholars have asserted that Esther is a "secular" book in which God plays no role.[19] While it is true that the absence of God's name is a curious feature, as we will see, it in no way indicates the absence of God in the story.

The nonappearance of God's name has been explained by numerous theories, including the idea that it was an intentional deletion to avoid the Name's profanation during the highly festive celebration of Purim. It has been asserted that the festival, known for its heavy drinking, was no time to pronounce the sacred name.[20] Other commentators see the book accentuating the human element of the story. The author wants to stress the role of human beings in shaping the course of history and their need to take individual responsibility.[21] Andre LaCocque avers that the author avoids any mention of the deity in a Persian setting because there is "a theology for the land of Israel and another for the Dispersion."[22] These along with other attempts to explain God's "hiddenness" in the story rarely deny that the book has a religious tone to it.[23] At the very least, as Michael V. Fox offers, there is the possibility that the author is seeking to convey "uncertainty about God's role in history."[24] The author is seeking to reflect that "there can be no definitive knowledge of the working of God's hand in history."[25] While Fox's exploration of religious doubt being reflected in the Esther document is a highly thoughtful and provocative approach to the issue of God's hiddenness in the text, it fails to convince because of all

19. See Fox, *Character and Ideology*, 235, for a synopsis.

20. Paton, *Esther*, 239.

21. Berg, "After the Exile."

22. LaCocque, *The Feminine Unconventional*, 62.

23. Fox, *Character and Ideology*, 237–47, explores various theories concisely but informatively.

24. Ibid., 247. This perspective is reflective of that of Walter Brueggemann's overall view of Old Testament theology. Brueggemann says, "the rhetoric of the Old Testament is characteristically *ambiguous and open* . . . So much is left unsaid that the reader is left uncertain." (Brueggemann, *Theology of the Old Testament*, 110 [emphasis original]).

25. Ibid.

the evidence in the book that genuinely seems to point to God's real presence in the events of which it speaks.

e. *Clues to God's Whereabouts*

i. *A veiled reference to divine sovereignty in 4:14?* There are allusions to God's presence in a number of places, most notably Esth 4:14 where Mordecai asserts that deliverance for the Jews will come from "another place" if not from Esther. While it might be debatable that he is referring to a divine initiative, such a position is highly tenable. The idea of God's presence with Israel in their exile reaches back to the exilic prophets themselves. This is a decisive theological perspective for the community. What comes into play at this point in their life is a return to the concept that Israel is a people not a place. This is a foundational perspective for the nation, going back to its Patriarchs, whom God constituted as a people long before they were established in a land. This most ancient of theological paradigms is what needs renewal in exilic life. The thought of the author of Mordecai's veiled reference to deliverance is rooted in a theological perspective that understands that God has a covenant with his people and he will not break it. This covenant transcends land. It is rooted in relationship, and thus Mordecai is sure that deliverance will come because Israel is a people in relationship with a trustworthy and sovereign God.[26]

ii. *The call to fasting:* We can further see the place of the divine presence in Esther's own plea for her people to set aside three days and nights for fasting on her behalf as she prepares to visit her husband the king and make her case for the salvation of the Jewish people (4:16). While the nature of the fast is not made explicitly religious in the text, there is ample evidence to demonstrate that fasting in the later Jewish tradition is a religious act.[27] Indeed, the tenor of the request is saturated with humility. Esther

26. Laniak, "Esther's *Volkcentrism*," 82.

27. See White, "Esther a Feminine Model," 162. She refers to the work of Wilhelm Vischer, *Esther*. Munich: C. Kaiser, 1937, 15.

recognizes that her hope of convincing the king to overturn Haman's plot is not in her hands alone; she needs the support of her people, and her God.

iii. *Coincidences and reversals*: Further, one may discern the presence of God in this story by the numerous "coincidences" that occur throughout it. First is the whole series of events that leads to Esther's being chosen as queen. Then in ch. 6 the king's insomnia leads to his discovery of Mordecai's unrewarded loyalty. Further instances are Haman's entrance into the court just as Ahasuerus is trying to think of a way to reward Mordecai (6:4); the king's return from the garden at the precise moment that Haman literally throws himself on Esther's mercy (7:8); Mordecai's elevation to vice-regent while Haman takes his place on the gallows that he had built especially for Mordecai (7:9–8:2); and most explicitly in 9:1 where matters were "turned around for the Jews." While the reluctance of the author to attribute any of these "coincidences" directly to God remains a mystery, as David Clines notes, taken together these chance occurrences have a cumulative effect. They demonstrate the guiding hand of God. Clines offers the opinion that divine control of the events is not hidden at all. It is stated indirectly but clearly by means of the many coincidences in the story.[28]

iv. *Mass "conversions" of Persians to Judaism*: The effects of Esther's actions seem to find their full expression in the eighth chapter when Mordecai is elevated to vice-regent and we are told that many people of "other nationalities" become Jews (8:17). This is a dramatic expression of the overall impact of Esther's actions. The fact that the people who "converted" did so as a result of "fear" of the Jews can be understood as a reflection of the expected response to a display of God's power (Deut 2:25; 11:25).[29]

28. Clines, *Esther Scroll,* 153.
29. Ibid., 89.

v. *God's absence as literary device and teaching technique*: The absence of God in Esther is a message in itself. The non-mention of the divine name acts as a literary device. It tells the readers that God is absent in a very overt way. It expresses the hiddenness of God in the midst of diasporic existence but recognizes that God is somehow still present even in his confusing absence. This is the fulcrum of hope for those in exile. God is never fully absent. Yahweh is "experienced" in his absence. His activity, or lack thereof, in the events of exile is still a part of his presence with the community of faith. Even if he is not near in immediate experience he is always in the background and his presence is experienced in less obvious, though still discernable, ways.[30]

f. *Canonization as a Key Interpretive Clue*

Scholars and readers of Esther through the centuries have argued over Esther's place in the Hebrew and Christian canon. These disputes have been based on both the historical and religious viability of the book.[31] The problem has been exacerbated by the variations in the text of Esther itself.[32] When Esther was definitively accepted into the Hebrew canon is not easy to determine, although it certainly began receiving acceptance in the second century BCE and found a secure place at some point in the first four centuries CE. Similarly, following much debate, its entrenchment in all Christian canons has been secure since at least the fifth century CE.[33]

Despite its tumultuous journey to canonicity, Esther is now safely ensconced among the books deemed to constitute Holy Scripture and for this reason must be read as such. This

30. For brief discussions on the concept of presence in absence see Terrien, *Elusive Presence*, 321–24, and Brueggemann, *Deep Memory, Exuberant Hope*, 82–83. Brueggemann sees the logic of the position but denies that it fully captures what is going on in the speech expressions of exilic texts.

31. For a helpful overview of this issue see ch. 1 in Berg, *Book of Esther*.

32. Investigation into the development of the Esther scrolls is outside the purview of this article. For a solid overview of these issues see Baldwin, *Esther*, 42–48.

33. For a detailed discussion see Bush, *Ruth, Esther*, 273–77.

locatedness of Esther in the biblical canon leads us to look for God in the text. Our interpretation of the book is, and should be, informed by the kind of literature that it is—biblical literature. Left outside of the canon it could well represent a secular vision for Jews in diaspora. However, as a part of Scripture it must be given a theological reading. It is this canonical location that calls us to read Esther as a sacred story and is the most vital reason for us to look for God in it. Just as those who made decisions regarding canonicity saw the theological value in the scroll so should modern readers approach the text with an eye for where God may be found in the text.

3. *The Sermon: Esther as a Homiletical Model*

Can Esther serve as a model for contemporary homiletics? If so, the question to be asked about the nature of the text is not "Why is God not mentioned in Esther?" but rather, "What is the author trying to do by not mentioning the name of God in Esther?"

Of course we will never be sure of the answer to this question; however, could it be a narrative device? Is it a way to communicate the sense of God's absence in exilic life? Has the author chosen to craft the narrative in a way that teaches both the absence and presence of God simultaneously? If so, can preachers do the same with the form of sermon they choose? Wisely applied, could a sermon that did not mention the name of God have a spiritually significant message that leaves a lasting impact on its hearers just as Esther has had on its readers for centuries now?

In order to answer this question in the affirmative several things need to be considered.

a. *Foundations for Esther as a Homiletical Model*

While Esther constitutes the only whole book in the Bible where the divine name is not mentioned, there are certainly other places in Scripture where a speaker engages in an act of proclamation intending to move people toward God or help them understand the nature of God, and yet does not mention the name of God. This is the case in Nathan's famous address to David in

2 Samuel 12. Nathan uses a parable to get the king's attention and demonstrate the unrighteousness of David's adultery with Bathsheba and his subsequent murder of her husband Uriah. The story of a rich man's misappropriation of a poor man's beloved sheep evoked from David the reaction, "As surely as the Lord lives, the man who did this must die!" (2 Sam 12:5 TNIV) The prophet's story, without mentioning the name of God, provoked a highly theological response. Further, it brought David to the realization of his own sin and drove him to genuine repentance. This story reminds us that a narrative without direct reference to the divine can still draw out divine responses.

In a similar way, the teaching of Jesus is marked, in his parables, by occasions where divine lessons are given in speech that decidedly lacks explicit reference to the name of God. Stories like the Parable of the Sower (Matt 13:3–9), the Good Samaritan (Luke 10:30–37), and the Lost Sheep, Lost Coin, and Lost Son (Luke 15) all lack any overt reference to God. This of course in no way denies that they contain lessons intended to teach people about God and fidelity to his ways; it is to recognize, however, that Jesus employed stories that referred to "secular" themes and not to the divine name in order to convey a message of divine consequence.[34]

Homileticians like Fred Craddock and Eugene Lowry have noted that Jesus' use of the narrative style, particularly in his use of parables, is a highly suggestive model for communicating the gospel in our day.[35] This leads us to recognize that Scripture

34. It is worth noting that several of Jesus' parables only mention God in a concluding phrase. See, for example, the parable of the shrewd manager (Luke 16:13). Other parables only mention God in the introductory phrase "the kingdom of God is like" (in Matthew it is "The kingdom of heaven is like"): see, for example, the parables of the Growing Seed and the Mustard Seed (Mark 4:26–32). It is quite accurate to say that most of Jesus' parables have no, or very limited, overt reference to the divine person.

35. See Lowry, *Doing Time in the Pulpit*, 28, 68–69; and Craddock, *Overhearing the Gospel*, 26.

itself uses stories that call the listener/reader to consider the ways of God without actually mentioning his name.[36]

b. *"Preaching Subversively" as an Effective Approach*

Utilizing a form of sermon that makes little or no direct reference to the name of God is an attempt to preach subversively. It tries to sneak up on the listeners and impart a lesson about God in an indirect way. It tries to help people experience the text rather than just understand it, to enter into the narrative and be captured by it, rather than stand outside of it as one trying to analyze it or "figure it out." This is not to diminish the need for people to understand the text; it is however to recognize that in today's postmodern, post-Christian culture, the need to experience a text often comes before the need and the ability to understand it. For those who have little or no understanding of the Christian faith, a story that refers directly to aspects of life that they are familiar with may provide a way to draw them into the story of the gospel without asking them to be conversant with the church's encoded language, which at times can keep people away from the gospel. For those who have heard the message a multitude of times it offers a fresh hearing of the message. Charles Campbell summarizes Fred Craddock when he writes, "more information is not what is necessary; what is needed is something else: an experience of information we already possess."[37] Indeed, an experience of the gospel is exactly what is needed by many hearers in these postmodern times. Lowry comments on Jesus' ability to use stories to answer individuals'

36. It can be argued that Jesus' parables are not as indirect as the story of Esther since they use very stock images (king, shepherd, banquet, etc.) in their narrative. These images had overt religious connotations, which made their function in the parable more easily recognizable. While this may be true, it certainly does not deny the effectiveness of Esther as a didactic narrative. In fact, in a culture that is increasingly biblically and religiously illiterate there are fewer and fewer terms that can be considered "stock" language. Thus, the indirectness of Esther may typify postmodern preaching of this sort even more clearly than Jesus' parables do.

37. Campbell, *Preaching Jesus*, 127.

questions so that they were transformed by the experience without realizing what was taking place. He writes,

> When asked a question, often right out of the vested interest of the questioner, he did not say: "Perhaps you should ask that another way" or "Here's the question you should have asked." He simply proceeded to tell a story—one that may or may not have appeared related to the question. The questioner could not get defensive, yet could not argue. One had to wait and see—and then it was too late![38]

As Jesus' questioners were drawn into the experience of the story, they were left with an altered perspective, one that left them seeing the situation differently. As we have already noted, Jesus often did this by using stories that did not even mention the name of God. For this reason, an approach that draws the audience into a narrative and subversively seeks to inculcate the values and perspectives of God's kingdom so that the congregation is effectively engaged into God's story is a viable approach, even if it does not include the divine name.

c. *A Scripturally Generated Approach to Narrative*

A criticism of narrative preaching has been that it is rooted in a liberal theological method that emphasizes experience at the heart of homiletics.[39] While it is clear that this is a well-founded criticism, it has often been based upon the charge that narrative preaching tends to be rooted in various narrative theories more than in the church's Scripture or particular biblical narratives.[40] The approach being suggested here stands in opposition to such charges and seeks to find narrative structures that are fully employed by the Scriptures themselves. As we will explore in the next major section, there are narrative practices that the author of Esther employs to accomplish the intended purpose. Similarly, a study of Jesus' parables can yield insight into what

38. Lowry, *Doing Time in the Pulpit*, 68–69.
39. Campbell, *Preaching Jesus*, 165.
40. Ibid., 167.

can rightly be called a scripturally-generated approach to narrative.[41]

Such an approach can begin with either a life experience or a biblical text. It may emanate from the preacher's desire to address an issue related to the current experience of her congregation. A text is chosen and a narrative is developed that faithfully communicates the theology of that text. At another time, the preacher may decide that an appropriate way to proclaim a given text is through a narrative that is exegetically sensitive and highly applicable to the congregation, yet accomplishes both these tasks in a highly subversive way, without invoking the divine name in the sermon. In both cases a narrative is constructed that seeks to intermingle human experience with biblical perspectives on that experience, ultimately seeking to interpret and shape that experience in a way that absorbs people's experience into the biblical view of the world. This is what the author of Esther seeks to do and it is also what Jesus does in his parables. The reality of life in this world generated the questions and issues to which the book of Esther spoke. The response of the main characters to their situations provided wise guidance as to how the original readers could respond to their ongoing diaspora, and offered clues as to where God was in the midst of what felt like his complete abandoning. Jesus spoke parables that began with questions posed directly out of a person's experience of life in this world.[42] He also spoke parables that came out of his own intention to declare the kingdom of God.[43]

In this way the genesis for a narrative that does not refer to God but still teaches about God can be either human experience or a biblical text. In each case its ultimate aim is to offer a theologically reflective approach to homiletics that speaks

41. An investigation of the narrative structure of parables is well outside the scope of this article, although Lowry, *How to Preach a Parable*, has certainly addressed the issue.

42. See, for example, the context for the three parables in Luke 15.

43. See, for example, the context for the parables in Matthew 13.

obviously and directly to human experience from a biblical perspective.

d. *Essential Practices for Using Esther as a Homiletical Model*
In order to maximize Esther as a homiletical model it is imperative that we understand some of the mechanisms present in and around the text that made it a powerful spiritual narrative for Israel. The following points seek to identify the things that were essential for the Esther narrative to find resonance with its original audience, and will also be essential to preaching in a way that is useful to contemporary audiences. I will also give examples from a sermon that I preached using this approach.

i. *Locatedness*: The sermon must have a narrative that is identifiable in its context; it must speak of things that the audience can readily identify with. This means that it either speaks concretely of life in this world as the audience knows it, or uses symbols and conventions familiar to them.

Esther was set in a place that had resonance with its readers: Susa was a real place, Xerxes was a king, and the Persians were their subjugators. These realities evoked the exilic experience and called out from the readers memories connected to identifiable people and places. If a narrative is inaccessible to people, any potential meaning it may have will be lost. A narrative sermon must serve its context by setting a scenario that is readily identifiable to its audience, either because it speaks about people and places they know or uses story-telling conventions that they understand. Further, they must be able to see themselves in the story and see how the narrative speaks to their situation in order for the message to have maximum effect.

I employed this technique in a sermon on the power of the Holy Spirit to enable Christians to live sanctified lives. I used a story of a beautiful, young, but physically unimposing princess, who was forced to go on a journey through dangerous, unfriendly territory on a mission to bring deliverance to her people. She was divinely enabled for the journey by a special gift given to her by an angel. This made her capable for the mission, although she had to venture out in faith and trust that what was put within her by the angel would be sufficient for the challenges she would face. This story employed conventional story-telling themes like a princess, a perilous journey, overwhelming odds, and a "secret" weapon that made the journey possible. These are devices that most people can readily identify and make connections with.

Part of the effectiveness of this approach comes from including the audience in the process of making meaning from a narrative. The audience become legitimate participants in the sermon process. They hear a story that speaks of things familiar to them, they understand that there is meaning in this story, and they begin to put the pieces together in their minds, constructing meaning from the story for their lives. Again, we have Jesus' teaching as an example of this approach. He constantly drew on common events, places, and experiences to construct a story and make his point, often trusting that his audience would get the religious meaning of a story without there being much, if any, reference to God. Craddock notes:

> The effectiveness of much of Jesus' preaching depended not simply on the revelatory power of his parables but also upon the perceptive power of those who attended to them. "Let anyone with ears to hear listen."[44]

Craddock points out that giving an audience "room to respond" marks a good drama. It is entirely appropriate to expect the audience to fill in the story and take responsibility for giving it part of its meaning.[45] This seems to be exactly what the author of Esther did by offering the community a narrative that affirmed both their role and God's in diasporic life without speaking directly about God or about how Israel was supposed to respond to the story. They were invited to enter the story and find God there. They were invited to take the wisdom provided by Esther and figure out how to embody it in their current diaspora.

This is possible because Esther speaks to its audience in concrete ways, using familiar terms and experiences, and then

44. Craddock, *As One without Authority*, 54.
45. Ibid.

invites them to see God in the story and discern how he may also be present in their lives.

ii. *Clues*: In aiding the audience to discern meaning and see God in a narrative devoid of his name, it is crucial to use clues that lead the hearer to deduce that seeing God in the narrative is the best explanation for it. For example, the use of actions and words that have religious overtones points to the activity of God in a narrative even if the name of God is never mentioned. Words, symbols, actions, "coincidences," and unexpected plot reversals all can point to a divine hand at work and are necessary narrative devices that lead the hearer to discern God in the story. As noted above, the writer of Esther employs such things liberally throughout the narrative.

Ronald Theimann points out that the Gospels employ a strategy not unlike the one suggested here. In the Gospels, God's direct involvement in the action is rarely depicted. Instead Jesus takes center stage and readers are invited to see the mighty work of God through the activities and words of this man.

> God's hiddenness is an essential part of the New Testament message, because the cumulative depiction of Jesus' identity brings an increasing convergence between the activity of Jesus and that of the hidden God of Israel. The connection between God's intention and Jesus' mission is announced explicitly in the baptism and transfiguration stories, but is established more subtly in the narrative sequence itself.[46]

Reading the Gospels through the lens of twenty centuries of history leads us to approach the text with many assumptions, both good and bad. However, for the original readers, the presence of God in the Gospels was largely to be discerned by reading (or hearing) the narrative and coming to conclusions based on what they found in the story of Jesus.

As a story offers its listeners (or readers) clues to guide them on their journey of deduction, the attentive audience member will discern what is going on in the story and begin making

46. Thiemann, *Revelation and Theology*, 89.

connections between the narrative and the hidden presence of God within it.[47]

In my sermon containing the story of the princess, I used many clear "coincidences" and occurrences that could only be explained by some kind of divine intervention. I also employed an angel as a character to further lead people to consider that the success of the princess's journey was clearly coming from forces outside of herself. In order to further help the audience make connections I portrayed the princess as very human: she experienced fear, doubt, and confusion while on her journey, just as we do on our faith journey as Christians. Further, her experiences bore resemblance to those we all face: temptation, intimidation, and trials.

iii. *The exemplary behavior of the main characters*: The story of Esther has didactic potency because the main characters, Esther and Mordecai, demonstrate the potential for Jewish life in exilic circumstances. Their behavior points to their faith and allegiance to the community and, one can assume, the God who formed the community. As Carol Bechtel points out in her commentary on Esther, one of the clear themes of the book is the distinction of Esther and Mordecai against King Ahasuerus and Haman. The extravagant and unwise lives of the latter are contrasted with the propriety of the former, and it becomes clear that Jewish piety wins out over Persian disproportion every time.[48]

In the same way, a narrative sermon that features characters who exemplify clear Christian attitudes and behavior over and against characters who exemplify distinctly non-Christian ones will point the audience toward the didactic nature of the sermon and help them to identify who the "heros" are, and, in turn, whom it is being suggested that they should seek to emulate.

Just as it is really not hard to distinguish in Esther who the "good guys" are, so a sermon that follows a similar narrative

47. See Hauwerwas and Burrell, "From System to Story," 179. The authors discuss the way the use of language and character can lead the audience to conclusions without "any need for philosophical reminders."

48. Bechtel, *Esther*, 7–10.

pattern can also clearly present ideal Christian behavior, faith, and patterns of living without mentioning the name of the divine One who establishes those patterns. Just as Esther functioned as a model for Jews who were untangling the complexities of living in a marginalized (or exilic) situation, so too does the church need (post) modern narratives that offer us exemplars of Christian life in the post-Christian context of contemporary society. A narrative sermon that offers a depiction of such characters can offer subversive wisdom for Christian living in a marginalized context.

In the sermon in which I used the princess story, the main character exhibited great faith in the idea that she had been divinely empowered for her journey. She trusted in the angel's word even though there was no physical evidence that she was different. This connects with our own challenge to trust the filling of God's Spirit despite any lack of obvious outward manifestation. She also exhibited noble character in that she accepted the mission given to her on behalf of her people who, without her help, would have been in great peril. This invites listeners to consider how they will respond to God's invitation to courageously engage their world in faith that the Spirit will enable them. These are ideal traits that invite listeners to consider how they will respond to the biblical text that the story is explicating.

iv. *The sermon as key interpretive clue*: Ultimately, it is Esther's place in the biblical canon that provokes us to look for God's presence in the story. As we have noted, the absence of the divine name has made Esther's place among the books of the Bible suspect for a justifiable reason. No one denies that Esther is a wonderful story that can entertain and enrich audiences of all ages, however, if it is taken out of its context within the biblical canon, its power as a theological story changes. The key to its theological viability is its place in the canon. Ultimately its location in the canon becomes its interpretive key.

In the same way, a narrative sermon that speaks about God without direct reference to God is highly dependent upon its locatedness as a message delivered from a Christian pulpit. Outside of the canon, Esther is easily understood as a secular story.

Within the canon, one can perceive God all through it. A story told at the local pub is just a good story; located in a Christian pulpit it is interpreted in a completely different way.

A message can, even should, be augmented by other elements in a church worship service. A biblical text that relates to and gives exegetical substance to the message may be read prior to the sermon; songs may be sung both before and after the message that relate to the theme of the message; prayers may be prayed that prepare the congregation for the message and lead them in a response to it.

These devices, added to the fact that the message is being proclaimed in a church, can provide the necessary context for a sermon that does not include the name of God to be understood as a message about God, just as Esther's place in the canon provides the key interpretive clue for it as a book that reveals the activity of a hidden God.

In the sermon I preached using the princess, the order of service before and after the sermon clearly pointed to a theme that related to the Holy Spirit and his empowering presence in our lives. Songs were chosen, the theme was described creatively near the beginning of the service, and prayers were crafted so as to point to the theme prior to the sermon. Also the text, Rom 8:1–13, was read right before the sermon was preached. After the sermon, a song focused on the Spirit that clearly invited a response to the sermon was sung, and a brief concluding statement that was both invitational and also covered over some of the rough theological edges potentially left unclarified by the story was offered before the final benediction drew the sermon and theme of the service together in a clear way.

Conclusion

An approach such as the one proposed here is a homiletical tool for a preacher to employ. Just as carpenters need various tools in their tool belts for specific jobs, so, too, preachers need various homiletical methods in order to preach creatively and with freshness over the long haul. This is especially true when one is preaching to the same congregation week after week. Preaching narrative sermons that do not mention God's name is not intended as the only method for a preacher to use, nor is it here suggested that it is the best model for any particular genre of Scripture. It is my proposal, however, that, when done properly, such a sermon can have enlightening effects on listeners in just the same way that Esther has provoked millions of readers over the centuries.

In these postmodern days, such an approach to preaching invites the congregants to be participators in the meaning-making of the message, and allows hearers to enter into the experience of the sermon by trusting them to "have ears to hear." It can provide a powerfully subversive approach to preaching in much the same way as Jesus' parables did (do). The point comes at the audience like a "sneak punch," or as entering through the "back door." The payoff is sometimes surprising and unexpected. Jesus obviously thought this could be a highly effective way to communicate as did the author of Esther.

For veteran church goers, familiar with the stories and doctrines of the Bible, the method provides a fresh hearing of Scripture, one that asks something of them rather than just reworks a familiar theme in a way similar to what has been done in the past. For those unfamiliar with the language of the Bible, it can open up the vistas of possibility and provide a precursor to further engagement with the gospel.

Above all, it provides the opportunity for the listener to experience the text. Stories, after all, are not about theories or themes, but what it is like to fall in love, go on a great adventure, or think that you have met God in one of life's circumstances.[49]

Preaching should provide listeners with opportunities to experience a text in surprising, even mystical, ways and when used effectively, even narratives that do not mention God's name can lead people into an experience of the divine.

49. See Hanson, *A Stay against Confusion*, 33.

Bibliography

Baldwin, Joyce. *Esther: An Introduction and Commentary.* TOTC. Downers Grove, IL: InterVarsity Press, 1984.

Bechtel, Carol M. *Esther.* Louisville KY: John Knox Press, 2002.

Berg, Sandra Beth. "After the Exile: God and History in the Books of the Chronicles and Esther." In *The Divine Helmsman,* edited by J. L. Crenshaw and S. Sandmel, 107–27. New York: Ktav, 1980.

———. *The Book of Esther: Motifs, Themes and Structures.* Missoula, MO: Scholars Press, 1979.

Bromley, Roger. *Narratives for a New Belonging: Diasporic Cultural Fictions.* Edinburgh: Edinburgh University Press, 2000.

Brueggemann, Walter. *Cadences of Home.* Atlanta: John Knox Press, 1997.

———. *Deep Memory, Exuberant Hope: Contested Truth in a Post Christian World.* Minneapolis: Fortress Press, 2000.

———. *Theology of the Old Testament: Testimony, Dispute, Advocacy.* Minneapolis: Fortress Press, 1997.

Bush, Frederic. *Ruth, Esther.* WBC. Waco, TX: Word, 1996.

Campbell, Charles L. *Preaching Jesus: New Directions for Homiletics in Hans Frei's Postliberal Theology.* Grand Rapids: Eerdmans, 1997.

Clines, David J. A. *The Esther Scroll: The Story of the Story.* JSOTSup 30. Sheffield: JSOT Press, 1984.

Craddock, Fred. *As One without Authority*. St. Louis: Chalice Press, 2001.

———. *Overhearing the Gospel*. Nashville: Abingdon Press, 1978.

Crites, Stephen. "The Narrative Quality of Experience." In *Why Narrative?: Readings in Narrative Theology*, edited by Stanley Hauerwas and L. Gregory Jones, 65–88. Eugene, OR: Wipf & Stock , 1997.

Fox, Michael V. *Character and Ideology in the Book of Esther*. Columbia: University of South Carolina Press, 1991.

Fulford, Robert. *The Triumph of Narrative*. Toronto: Anansi Press, 1999.

Hanson, Ron. *A Stay against Confusion: Essays on Faith and Fiction*. New York: Harper Collins, 2001.

Hauwerwas, Stanley and David Burrell. "From System to Story." In *Why Narrative?: Readings in Narrative Theology*, edited by Stanely Hauerwas and L. Gregory Jones, 158–90. Eugene, OR: Wipf & Stock, 1997.

Humphries, W. Lee. "A Life-style for Diaspora: A Study of the Tales of Esther and Daniel." *JBL* 92 (1973) 211–23.

Jackson, Phillip W. "On the Place of Narrative in Teaching." In *Narrative in Teaching, Learning, and Research*, edited by Hunter McEwan and Kieran Egan, 3–23. New York: Teachers College Press, 1995.

LaCocque, Andre. *The Feminine Unconventional: Four Subversive Figures in Israel's Tradition*. Minneapolis: Fortress Press, 1990.

Laniak, Tim. "Esther's *Volkcentrism* and the Reframing of Post-Exilic Judaism." In *The Book of Esther in Modern Research*, edited by Sidnie White Crawford and Leonard J. Greenspoon, 77–90. London: T. & T. Clark, 2003.

Lowry, Eugene. *Doing Time in the Pulpit.* Nashville: Abingdon Press, 1985.

———. *How to Preach a Parable: Designs for Narrative Sermons.* Nashville: Abingdon Press, 1989.

Morgan, Donn F. *Between Text and Community: The "Writings" in Canonical Interpretation.* Minneapolis: Fortress Press, 1990.

Paton, Lewis B. *The Book of Esther.* ICC. Edinburgh: T&T Clark, 1908.

Smith, Daniel. *Religion of the Landless: The Social Context of the Babylonian Exile.* Bloomington, IN: Myer-Stone Books, 1989.

Smith-Christopher, Daniel. *A Biblical Theology of Exile.* Minneapolis: Fortress Press 2002.

Talmon, S. "Wisdom in the Book of Esther." *VT* 13 (1963) 419–55.

Terrien, Samuel. *The Elusive Presence: Toward a New Biblical Theology.* San Francisco: Harper & Row, 1978.

Thiemann, Ronald. *Revelation and Theology: The Gospel as Narrated Promise.* Notre Dame: University of Notre Dame Press, 1985.

White, Sidnie Ann. "Esther a Feminine Model for Jewish Diaspora." In *Gender and Difference in Ancient Israel*, edited by Peggy L. Day, 161–73. Minneapolis: Fortress Press, 1989.

[*MJTM* 10 (2008–2009) 101–39]

Participating in Godliness: A Study of the Laws concerning the Socially Marginalized in the Torah

Jamie Hussain
McMaster Divinity College, Hamilton, ON

How does the average twenty-first century Christian seeking out the compassion of God relate to a God who decreed that widows and orphans be invited to dinner at the end of every third year (Deut 14:29)? How does a law that prescribed two turtledoves as an offering to atone for a new mother's uncleanness (Lev 12:8) comfort a new Christian mother trying to make the next month's rent? Does an understanding of God's laws regarding the fair treatment of one's slave (Exod 21) give the Christian any relevant direction regarding ethical conduct in a country where slavery is no longer legal?

God is often perceived by Christians to be dichotomous, a view that distinguishes between the God of the Old Testament and the God of the New. Such an erroneous concept has a negative impact on the practice of Christians and their pastors. The New Testament is read and reread, preached and re-preached, while the Old Testament is left on the shelf. Neither is then understood as they potentially could be. Yet a careful reading of the Old Testament reveals that the One who delivered the Sermon on the Mount is the same One who delivered the Ten Commandments from Mount Sinai.

The following study will entail a canonical approach to the laws of the Torah that govern Israel's treatment towards their most vulnerable population, the socially marginalized. Through these laws, the compassion of God becomes vivid.[1] God is

1. While I acknowledge that the whole of Scripture is comprised of texts written in different times, places, and cultures, the goal of this study is not to

revealed through Mosaic Law, that portion of the Old Testament that Christians turn to the least and find most irrelevant, as a God who is concerned for and involved in human affairs. The social justice laws in the Torah function as a revelation of God's compassion, a godly characteristic that not only was to be reflected through the practical behavior of ancient Israel, but also by all his people in covenant with him, regardless of the culture or century in which they live.[2]

This study will also reveal three primary themes arising from the laws about the socially marginalized. Arising from each law is the practical theme of provision, protection, or inclusion. As the Israelites obeyed these laws they would have found themselves providing these vulnerable ones with the basic necessities of life such as food and clothing. Obedience to these laws also meant that the Israelites would protect them from injustice in the courts and ensure they were included in the annual feasts and times of worship. In so doing, the Israelites were working out practically the compassion that God has for the socially marginalized in society. As the Bible is the revelation of God, so these laws concerning the socially marginalized are a revelation of God's compassion.

After outlining the varying socially marginalized groups as named in the Torah, I will present a summary of the laws concerning them within the context of the law code in which they are found, giving particular attention to the theological motivations behind the laws. The summaries will also include the functional themes that arise from each law, citing samples from each law code. The study will conclude with some observations about how this material relates to New Testament teaching and to Christian life today.

propose historical human sources from which the laws arose. It focuses on the laws in their final form, which attest that the Lord is their source.

2. Hamilton, *Social Justice and Deuteronomy*, 157.

The Socially Marginalized in the Torah

Israel's socially marginalized people are the ones who would not have belonged to one of the "primary units in the ancient Israelite social organization."[3] This *beth 'av* ("house of the father") unit was the basic community unit and was headed by the father. The extended family that was included in this *beth 'av* "was made up of as many sets of childbearing adults and their dependants as was necessary for the entire group to feed and protect itself."[4] To be outside, or marginalized from, this basic social support unit of provision and protection was to be at risk. The identities of "socially marginalized people" are given in the laws as the orphan, widow, foreigner, and slave, and collectively as the poor.

Not every orphan and widow (Exod 22:22–24; Deut 10:18; 14:29; 16:11; 24:17–21; 26:12–13; 27:19) was poor, however. In early Israelite society women and children needed "the protection and economic support of an adult male."[5] If, due to war or disease or some other mortal fate, a family lost the male providing that support, a widow and her now fatherless child, or orphan, could turn to the deceased's family or the widow's family for that protection and economic support. Subsequently, despite being widowed or orphaned, they could end up being well provided for. Otherwise a widow and orphan "were destitute if they had no household to provide them support and nurture,"[6] and thus would be in real danger of being taken advantage of or even abused by others, and of starvation.

This was the case for the foreigner (Exod 22:21; 23:9, 12; Num 9:14; 15:14–16; 35:15; Lev 17:8–9, 15–16; 18:26; 19:9–10, 33–34; 20:2; 22:18–19; 23:22; 24:16, 22; 25:6, 23; Deut 1:16; 10:17b–19; 14:21, 29; 24:17–18; 27:19; 28:43; 31:12) as well. While it was possible for a foreigner to prosper in Israel, this was the exception, not the rule. Whether non-Hebrews were passing through or living in Israel, they were at risk of being exploited as

3. McNutt, *Reconstructing the Society*, 216.
4. Mathews and Benjamin, *Social World*, 7.
5. Malchow, "Social Justice in the Israelite Law Codes," 301.
6. Perdue, "The Israelite and Early Jewish Family," 194.

was any foreigner in a strange land. Not only would there always be the potential for ethnically motivated abuse, they could never permanently own land. "Without inherited land, a sojourner could not sit among the elders and may not have been allowed to institute suits before the court and thus was vulnerable to exploitation, fraud, and social ostracism."[7] Thus, most non-Hebrews living in Israel served as "hired laborers"[8] of the *beth 'av* unit, and were dependant on their daily wage for survival.

It was not only the foreigner, but the Israelite as well, who had the potential of falling into a life of slavery in Israel (Exod 21:2–11, 20–21, 26–27; 23:12; Lev 25:6, 35–55; Deut 23:15–16). While both foreign and Israelite bondservants are called "slaves" in the law, there is a type of slavery to which the foreigner was subjected that the Israelite was not. It is likely that the foreigner either became a slave by being purchased as such or became one by being taken captive in war. As such, the foreigner's form of slavery was "a genuine slavery."[9] If, however, Israelites fell into slavery, it was most likely due to financial indebtedness. To pay off the debt parents could sell one of their children into "temporary debt servitude and slavery."[10] They could also sell themselves into slavery. In this case the arrangement was as follows: "instead of signing a mortgage on his property he turned it over to the creditor . . . and by farming it himself gradually worked out of his indebtedness."[11] Additionally, the Israelite slave was to be treated less harshly than the foreign slave.

All those people who identified themselves as widow, orphan, foreigner, or slave, were not part of the typical landowning familial social structure that sustained and secured a person's life necessities. Since "wealth came from the land"[12] and they did not own land, they were dependant upon those *beth 'av* land-

7. Patrick, *Old Testament Law*, 86.
8. Perdue, "The Israelite and Early Jewish Family," 198.
9. North, *Sociology*, 2.
10. Perdue, "The Israelite and Early Jewish Family," 195–96.
11. North, *Sociology*, 2.
12. de Vaux, *Ancient Israel*, 72.

owning units for their survival. These socially marginalized people without a landowning family to take them in would remain continually at risk of being exploited and oppressed in their poverty-stricken state, and dependent on the generosity of others to ease that oppression. The disenfranchised widow, orphan, foreigner, and slave were all poor (Exod 22:25–27; 23:3, 6, 10–11; Lev 14:21–22; 19:15; 25:23–55; Deut 15:4–11; 24:12–15) and, therefore, depended on their neighbors daily for their survival. To ensure that these socially marginalized people were cared for, God included in the Torah laws that were specifically concerned with their well-being.

The Book of the Covenant

The first of the law codes in the Torah is the Book of the Covenant or Covenant Code. While these terms refer to Exod 20:22—23:33, they imply that at least part of the text "was a portion of an independent legal collection or law code before being incorporated into the Bible."[13] While there may be laws in the Book of the Covenant that had a pre-Sinai existence as well as counterparts in other foreign legal texts, the present shape of Exodus identifies Sinai as the place where God first gave his covenant people the laws that determined how they were to live before their God. Regardless of the source theories, in the end, the Book of the Covenant exists as a legal body of text within the canonical Torah.

Prior to the giving of the Sinai law, the Lord invited Moses and Aaron to ascend the mountain. However Moses warned, "do not let the priests and the people break through to come up to the LORD, or he will break forth upon them" (Exod 19:24). Then, after the law was given to the people and accepted by them, there was a sacrificial ceremony that concluded with Moses and Aaron once again going up before the Lord. This time, however, they went up with Aaron's sons Nadab and Abihu and seventy of Israel's elders, and on the mountain "they saw the God of Israel; . . .Yet he did not stretch out his hand against the nobles of the

13. Sprinkle, *Book of the Covenant*, 27.

sons of Israel; and they saw God, and they ate and drank" (Exod 24:9–11). The laws of Sinai had become binding on the two covenant parties, God and Israel, and thus they shared a new relationship based on the laws that determined the expected behavior of each.

Some of those behavioral expectations placed on the Israelites involved their treatment of the socially marginalized. It is here in the material that lies between the Decalogue in ch. 20 and the ceremony in ch. 24 that this Book of the Covenant addresses socially marginalized persons: the slave, foreigner, widow, orphan, and the poor.

Theological Motivations

When God began to give Israel the law, he did so without any mediator, speaking directly to the nation of Israel from Sinai. His first words were, "I am the LORD your God, who brought you out of the land of Egypt, out of the house of slavery" (Exod 20:2). Thus, as Israel listens to God they are first reminded "of the state of grace in which they stand."[14] The authority of the laws that follow then is based on God's self-identity as the Lord, and his act of grace, liberating Israel from the oppression of Egypt. Patrick explains this thought well when he writes:

> His deed demonstrated that he is worthy of the benefactors' allegiance. He is a God to whom they can entrust their fate. His commandments can be trusted to be an expression of his gracious will toward his people. The people can be expected to obey out of trust in the goodness of what he commands and out of gratitude for all his saving benefits.[15]

The motivation for Israel to obey these laws, then, is the relationship that God initiated with Israel, and not simply the law itself. Not only is Israel's past experience of God's grace in delivering them from oppression an overarching motivation for

14. Dumbrell, *Covenant and Creation*, 91.
15. Patrick, *Old Testament Law*, 42.

all the laws, but also certain laws draw on Israel's past experience that becomes a motivation for present practice.

For example, Exod 22:21 and 23:9 are two laws that prohibit the oppression of foreigners. In both cases it is Israel's past as oppressed foreigners themselves that is the stated reason they are not to oppress the foreigners in their land. The latter verse, however, adds the motivation "since you know the life of the foreigner" (23:9). The appeal here is to Israel's exodus experience and they are thus exhorted to "pity the deprived because in Egypt the Israelites learned how the needy feel."[16] In addition to reminding Israel of their past and appealing to a sense of empathy, Israel is pressed here to "care for the weak out of gratitude for God's deliverance."[17] Having been oppressed foreigners themselves and thus knowing the suffering that is inherent in such a life, Israel is to behave toward the foreigners under their rule as God did with them. Israel's exodus experience and God's involvement therein is therefore used as grounds for having such a law.

In the chart below, each law about the socially marginalized is listed in the order it appears in the text, as well as by the specific socially marginalized group that is named in that law. The "X" represents the resulting primary theme that results in the practical application of that particular law.

16. Malchow, *Social Justice*, 28.
17. Ibid.

Text of Law Exodus	Socially Marginalized Addressed	Primary Themes		
		Protection	Provision	Inclusion
21:2–6	Slave	X		
21:7–11	Slave	X		
21:16	Slave	X		
21:20–21	Slave	X		
21:26–27	Slave	X		
22:21	Foreigner	X		
22:22–24	Widow/ Orphan	X		
22:25–27	Poor	X		
23:3	Poor	X		
23:6	Poor	X		
23:9	Foreigner	X		
23:10–11	Poor		X	
23:12	Slave/ Foreigner			X

Functional Themes

The laws in the Book of the Covenant that govern Israel's treatment of the socially marginalized serve the socially marginalized in three ways. They protect them from harm or injustices, provide for their basic life necessities, or include them in community. Here in the Book of the Covenant the dominant recurring theme is of *protection* from abuse. The theme of protection arises from all the laws listed here, except the last two that have as their themes *provision* of food and *inclusion* in society. While one, two, or all three themes may arise from more than one of these laws, there is usually one primary theme or function the law serves on behalf of the marginalized individuals with which the law is concerned. For example, the first law concerns slaves who are to be freed after six years of servitude. Thus the slaves are protected from a lifetime of slavery. Upon the slave's release, the status of full citizen is restored and thus the former slave is included back into society. The last law, Exod 23:12, provides another example. Here every seventh day is declared a day of rest for everyone, including slaves. Thus, the slave has been included with the rest of the household and is thereby protected from being overworked; the slave is treated the same as everyone else.

An example of the intense concern and advocacy God has for the vulnerable is made clear in Exod 22:22–27. This text contains two laws that recall Israel's cry to God out of their oppression and his personal intervention of grace. The law's explicit concern is for the protection of the widow, orphan, and poor person. The first law prohibits the exploitation of a widow or orphan (vv. 22–24). If they are caused to suffer further at the hand of others, they may give out a "cry of distress"[18] to God, causing him to advocate on their behalf. Such a cry arouses the anger of God against the offending party, to whom God says, "then I will kill you with the sword so your wives will be widows and your sons will be orphans" (Exod 22:24). The second law also protects, as it prohibits a person's cloak, used as collateral for a loan, from being kept past evening (vv. 25–27). If someone must spend the night without a warm covering because of another, God will also hear that person's cry.

This cry is the same "cry of distress"[19] with which Israel called out to God when enslaved in Egypt. God heard their outcry and told Moses, "(I) have given heed to their cry because of their taskmasters, for I am aware of their sufferings. So I have come down to deliver them from the power of the Egyptians" (Exod 3:7–8). In addition to the widows and orphans, this direct appeal to God is also afforded to the "indebted neighbor" who must sleep without his pledged cloak (Exod 22:26–27), the "poor brother" who is refused a loan (Deut 15:9), and the "hired servant" whose wages are not paid to him at the end of the day (Deut 24:15). In all four cases the direct appeals to God are afforded only to socially marginalized people who suffer at the hands of others and therefore are in need of protection. While the cry in Exod 22:26–27 results in the assurance of being heard by God, the two cries to God in Deuteronomy result in the offense being counted as sin against the offender. In Exod 22:24, however, such a cry results in the aroused anger of God. The only other law that, when broken, results in the anger of God is the law against idolatry (Deut 6:14–15). In both of these cases,

18. Brown et al., *Hebrew Lexicon,* 858.
19. Ibid.

God's anger ultimately results in the death of the offender. Since the penalty of death is prescribed here for causing a widow or orphan to cry out, the surrounding community members would be highly motivated to afford sufficient benevolence. In the entire Book of the Covenant this is the only place where the Lord says, "I will kill" (Exod 22:24). Israel is thus urged to be compassionate to those who need compassion because the God with whom they are in covenant relationship is compassionate and was compassionate to them.[20]

Such laws are however "only illustrative"[21] and are to be extended out "into every sphere of life where injustice might be encountered."[22] The same is true not only for the rest of the Book of the Covenant but also for the Decalogue, the call of which is to "translate faith into action."[23] Such action is the prescribed behavior outlined by the laws of the Sinai covenant, mandated by the authority of God, self-binding upon Israel through their voluntary acceptance of the covenant, reflective of the character of God, and exemplified by the Exodus, which "became the model for God's willingness to save suffering people."[24]

Having now established a relationship with God, Israel was expected to obey the law through which that covenant relationship was established. Embedded in the law itself are reminders of their past oppression and the grace and compassion of God of which they were recipients when he delivered them from that oppression. God's covenant people were motivated to obey the law of God not only out of thankfulness to God for acting compassionately and graciously to them. As a people bound in covenant to God, their behavior ought to portray the characteristics of that God they served. As Israel obeyed the laws their behavior would in fact portray God's behavior. As demonstrated above,

20. Malchow, *Social Justice*, 28.
21. Fretheim, *God and World*, 248.
22. Ibid.
23. Dumbrell, *Covenant and Creation*, 91.
24. Malchow, *Social Justice*, 6.

those who obeyed the laws about the socially marginalized would demonstrate God's compassion and grace in practical ways. Depending on the law being obeyed, they would be attending to the vulnerable among them by protecting them, providing for them, or including them in mainstream society. These three themes demonstrate the practical ways God behaves towards his people, and subsequently, how those who call themselves his people ought to behave, based on their covenant relationship to God and the compassion God has shown them.

The Priestly Code Part I
(excluding The Holiness Code, Leviticus 17–27)

Having established the covenant relationship with Israel (Exod 20–24), the Lord provides the laws and instructions in preparation for his dwelling among his people. These laws govern the building of the tabernacle, the making of sacrifices, the installation of the priesthood, cleanness within the camp, the organization of the camp, and responsibilities for the Levites. Within these laws, which begin in Exodus 25 and continue though Leviticus and into Numbers, are the laws that address the socially marginalized.

Theological Motivations

God provided ethical examples of how to reflect the behavior of God toward the socially marginalized, which was a requirement for his people: "For I am the LORD your God. Consecrate yourselves therefore, and be holy, for I am holy" (Lev 11:44). This call to the people of Israel to be godly in their behavior is also connected in the following verse with his deliverance of Israel from Egypt. "For I am the LORD who brought you up from the land of Egypt to be your God; thus you shall be holy, for I am holy" (Lev 11:45). For Won W. Lee, the Priestly Code has Sinai as its origin[25] and is thus theologically motivated, as the Book of the Covenant is, by God's first words to the nation: "I am the LORD your God, who brought you out of the land of Egypt, out

25. Lee, *Punishment and Forgiveness*, 99

of the house of slavery" (Exod 20:2). Even as God's first words spoken directly to the people at Sinai tied together God's self-identity with the people's deliverance from Egypt, so too here in Lev 11:44–45, the authority of God is linked to "the relationship that exists between God and the Israelites."[26] Thus the Lord's gracious act of delivering Israel from the oppression of Egypt continues to be the theological motivation behind the laws.

Here among the Priestly laws, excluding the Holiness Code, God made laws that specifically sought to include those who would have otherwise remained excluded. If God who is holy makes provisions for the socially marginalized, then most certainly his covenant people, who are called to behave according to his holiness, ought to likewise concern themselves with the socially marginalized. If God's covenant people were going to live according to the law of God and reflect his holy character, they would have to afford the same grace to the socially marginalized as God did for them when he liberated them from slavery.

As with the Book of the Covenant, the laws that involve the socially marginalized have a recurring theme. While the main theme of the laws about the socially marginalized in the Book of the Covenant is protection, here it is primarily inclusion. Again, as with the Book of the Covenant, these laws are subject to secondary or tertiary themes of protection or provision. In the chart below, "X" represents the primary theme or function the law serves for the marginalized.

26. Malchow, *Social Justice*, 27.

Text of Law	Socially Marginalized Addressed	Primary Themes		
		Protection	Provision	Inclusion
Leviticus				
5:7, 11	Poor			X
12:8	Poor			X
14:21–22, 32	Poor			X
Numbers				
9:14	Foreigner			X
15:14–16	Foreigner			X
15:26–31	Foreigner			X
35:15	Foreigner			X

Functional Themes

If any of the Israelites became unclean, they were prohibited from fully participating in the community of worship. The stipulations one must follow to become clean again are mandated here in the Priestly Code by God. God provided a way for his people to once again be considered clean and therefore fully eligible members of the worship community. Yet, there were those who were in danger of forever remaining outside the worship community because they were too poor to meet the requirements that would make them clean.

Examples of God's concern for the inclusion of poor are the laws of Lev 5:7, 11. Here the law ensured that the poor and the poorest of the poor were not excluded from the community of worship because of their economic plight. It involved a "guilt offering" for the guilt incurred through the actions listed in vv. 1–4. They include refusing to testify, becoming unclean by touching an unclean thing or person, and making oaths thoughtlessly. The consequence of these actions is one of guilt. The guilty party has committed a sin and the process of forgiveness begins in v. 5. The guilty must confess (v. 5), and then make an offering of a female lamb or goat (v. 6).

The law of v. 7 is for those people who are poor and therefore do not own or are not able to obtain the required offering. Here a provision is made allowing for a substitute offering of two turtledoves or two sons of a dove. The priests then do their part as instructed in vv. 8–10, and the sin is forgiven (v. 10). In this way the poor are not excluded from being forgiven.

The law of v. 11 is for those people who are poor in the extreme, so much so that they do not have or cannot obtain the permitted substitute offering. The law also provides for them a further substitute offering of flour equal to one day's bread for one person.[27] From the richest in the land to the very poorest, no one was excluded from the opportunity to be forgiven for one of the four infractions above. Exceptions were made with regard to the required guilt offerings, ensuring that the poor also were included with everyone else in having atonement made for their sins. In doing so they were protected from remaining guilty and being ostracized.

God made sure the laws did not exclude people from coming to worship him. Likewise, through the law, God also ensured that resident foreigners and even lepers (14:21–22, 32) were not excluded from coming to worship him. These laws that make concessions for the poor, or specify the inclusion of the resident non-Hebrew, are examples of God's attitude, and how God's covenant people may practically reflect that attitude toward the socially marginalized in society.

Through the law of Leviticus, God continued to motivate Israel by reminding them of their past oppression and their personal experience of God's compassionate and gracious act of deliverance. God did so by explicitly stating, "For I am the LORD who brought you up from the land of Egypt to be your God," and then directed them, "thus you shall be holy, for I am holy" (Lev 11:45). Again, out of thankfulness to God, and because he had entered a covenant with them, Israel was to be like him. God's people were to behave in a "godly" manner. One way to do so was through obedience to the laws. As they obeyed the laws concerning the socially marginalized, Israel would bestow the same compassion upon others as God had bestowed on them as a nation. God included them unto himself through a covenant relationship, and by obeying the law in Leviticus Israel would

27. Milgrom, *Leviticus 1–16*, 306.

ensure that the poor were included with the rest of the nation in the worship of God. As God included others unto himself in covenant, so also his covenant people ought to ensure that they were not only not excluding, but actively including, those who are at risk of being left out of the wider worship community. Thus they, like God, would be applying godliness in practical ways shown forth through provision, protection, and inclusion of others.

The Priestly Code Part II: The Holiness Code: Leviticus 17–27

The Holiness Code is so named for its main theme of holiness. It appears in Leviticus 17–26, and throughout God repeats to the Israelites the phrases, "You shall be holy, for I the LORD your God am holy" (19:2), and "I am the LORD who sanctifies you" (20:8). "This idea, rarely encountered in the rest of Leviticus, is here stated repeatedly and emphatically," notes Levine.[28] Not only is there a distinctive theme to the Holiness Code but, in comparison to chs. 1–16, it differs in structure, vocabulary, style, and theology.[29] Nevertheless, despite its distinctive qualities the Holiness Code remains a work within the Priestly Code.[30]

The laws in the Holiness Code concerned specifically with the socially marginalized do not name the widow and orphan, as they do in the Book of the Covenant. The ones that are named in the Holiness Code are the resident foreigner, the slave, the poor, and the afflicted. The descriptions "poor" and "afflicted," however, probably included the "widow and orphan," since they most certainly would have been among the most poor and afflicted in society.

Theological Motivations

There are two key theological motivations found in the Holiness Code. Those motivations are related to God as the one who

28. Levine, *Leviticus*, 111.
29. Milgrom, *Leviticus 17–22*, 1319.
30. Knohl, *Sanctuary of Silence*, 1.

delivered Israel out of their oppression in Egypt and God's command to be holy.

The Holiness Code links reference to Israel's experience in Egypt to God's identity as the one who delivered them from their oppression. When the statement "I am the LORD your God" (Lev 18:2, 4, 30; 19:3, 4, 10, 25, 31, 34; 20:24; 23:22, 43; 24:22; 25:17; 26:1) is found by itself, it usually occurs as the concluding statement of a particular law or list of laws. The significance of this is found in the call of Moses where God announces himself to Moses as "YHWH" (Exod 3:13–14). Whether the name literally means "I am who I am," "I will be who I will be," or "I create what I create,"[31] when God gave to Moses his name "the deity had given himself to the worshippers concerned in commitment and trust."[32] Further, Dumbrell suggests that the name and character of God given to Moses will be revealed "by his future acts, particularly from the now imminent liberation. Moses is thus commissioned to go back to Egypt with this name which is now understood to be an indication of Yahweh's intention."[33] Thus, when a law or laws are attached to the statement "I am the LORD" it carries the authority and the mark of the one who heard Israel's cry in Egypt (Exod 3:7), initiated their rescue through Moses, and identified himself as "the LORD, the God of your fathers, the God of Abraham, the God of Isaac, and the God of Jacob" (Exod 3:15).

While some of the laws about the socially marginalized have "I am the LORD your God" as a motivation embedded directly in the law, it is an overarching motivation of the entire Holiness Code. It begins in ch. 17 with "speak to Aaron and to his sons and to all the sons of Israel and say to them, 'This is what the LORD has commanded, saying,'" (v. 2), and ends in 26:46 with "These are the statutes and ordinances and laws which the LORD established between himself and the sons of Israel through

31. Dumbrell, *Covenant and Creation*, 83.

32. Ibid., 82.

33. Ibid., 84.

Moses at Mount Sinai." The source of Leviticus 17–26 is identified, at its beginning and at its end, as Yahweh.

Throughout the Holiness Code, varying forms of the words, "I am the LORD your God" (Lev 19:36; 22:33; 23:43; 25:38, 42, 55; 26:13, 45), are attached to varying forms of "who brought you out of the land of Egypt to give you the land of Canaan and to be your God" (Lev 25:38). When God identifies himself by name "his authority stands behind the promises or commands."[34] When he adds to this self-identity his act of freeing Israel from Egyptian oppression he "establishes the basis on which he expects them to accept his authority."[35]

Looking back now from Sinai, God had delivered Israel just as he told Moses he would, and thus, as Jansen says, "the one God who has revealed himself under the name Yahweh (Exod 3:13–16; 6:2–7) has filled that name with meaning as he redeemed Israel (Exod 20:2)."[36] Whether God's name "the LORD" is found in the text coupled with his act of rescuing Israel, or it is found by itself, "these laws are not self-contained or self-interpreting, but are covered by the story that fills the name Yahweh with content."[37]

In addition to "I am the LORD your God" as an overarching motivation for the laws of the Holiness Code, one finds the phrase: "be holy, for I the LORD your God am holy" (19:1; 20:7, 26; 21:8). Even though much of "being holy" concerned the specifics involved when approaching to worship God, "justice and compassion, too, were a dimension of holiness."[38] The ethical laws in the Holiness Code emphasize that ethical living, which involves the treatment of the socially marginalized, is "inextricably wedded"[39] to the rituals of holy worship. Thus every time a law concerning the socially marginalized appears in a law code, as it does in each law code, the ethical and moral

34. Tigay, *Deuteronomy*, 63.
35. Ibid.
36. Janzen, *Old Testament Ethics*, 97.
37. Ibid., 68.
38. Levine, *Leviticus*, xi.
39. Balentine, *Leviticus*, 142.

dimension of God's holiness is presented. Thus the repeated proclamation "be holy for I am holy" became possible only "through observance of the cultic laws along with practice of just ways of love of neighbor and the stranger."[40]

As with the Book of the Covenant and the rest of the Priestly Code, the laws that involve these socially marginalized people in the Holiness Code have a recurring theme. While the main theme of the laws about the socially marginalized in the Book of the Covenant is *protection,* these laws in the Holiness Code continue with the main theme of *inclusion* that was begun in the previous portion of the Priestly Code. Again, as with the previous laws, each of these that thus far show themes of *protection, provision,* or *inclusion,* have one theme that primarily serves the socially marginalized, but also may reflect secondary or tertiary themes.

Text of Law Leviticus	Socially Marginalized Addressed	Primary Themes		
		Protection	Provision	Inclusion
17:8–9	Foreigner			X
17:10–14	Foreigner			X
17:15–16	Foreigner			X
18:26	Foreigner			X
19:9–10	Foreigner/Poor		X	
19:15	Poor	X		
19:33–34	Foreigner	X		
20:2	Foreigner			X
22:18–19	Foreigner			X
23:22	Foreigner/Poor		X	
24:16	Foreigner			X
24:22	Foreigner	X		
25:6	Foreigner/Poor		X	
25:24–55	Foreigner/Poor/ Slave	X		

Functional Themes

The primary theme or function served, running through the laws about the socially marginalized in the Priestly Code is *inclusion.*

40. Knohl, *Sanctuary of Silence*, 216.

While in the first portion of the Priestly Code it is exclusively *inclusion*, here in the Holiness Code it is predominantly so, occupying half the relevant laws. The other themes of *provision* and *protection* occupy the remainder.

What is unique to the laws about the socially marginalized in the Holiness Code is their focus on one segment of the socially marginalized population. Of the fourteen laws, thirteen name the foreigner as the object of the primary theme. The main concern of the Holiness Code, with regards to Israel's socially marginalized, is the foreigner. Whether the law primarily stipulates Israel's *provision*, *protection*, or *inclusion*, its primary object here is the foreigner. An example of each theme is provided below.

Leviticus 19:9–10 has, as its primary theme, *provision*. This law stipulates that when the field or vineyard is harvested it is not to be completely harvested. Some is to remain. This is another version of the law found in Exod 23:10–11 as part of the Book of the Covenant. Here, however, the law applies to any time a harvest takes place rather than only during the seventh year. Also, in addition to the poor, this law includes the foreigner as one of those towards whom this law will encourage provision. This law occurs within a list of a variety of laws that comprise ch. 19. The Lord introduces these laws with "speak to all the congregation of the sons of Israel and say to them, 'You shall be holy, for I the LORD your God am holy'" (v. 2) (the exhortation for which the Holiness Code is named). Embedded within this specific law itself is the phrase "I am the LORD your God." The implication of this for Milgrom is that "YHWH is the protector of the defenseless, and only those who follow his lead can achieve holiness."[41] Providing the poor and the foreigner the opportunity to gather their own food is to act in accordance with, and on behalf of, the heart of God. Finally, the list of laws of which Lev 19:9–10 is a part concludes with the "covenant formula,"[42] "I am the LORD your God" in 19:36.

41. Milgrom, *Leviticus 17–22*, 1624.

42. Wenham, *Leviticus*, 251.

Leviticus 19:33–34 is an example of a law prescribing *protection*. Here the Israelites were to treat the foreigner as they would one of their own citizens.[43] They were not only to withhold their hand from oppressing the foreigner, but were to reach out their hand to the foreigner with love. This is similar to a law just prior, "you shall love your neighbor as yourself; I am the LORD" (Lev 19:18). This law follows "You shall be holy, for I the LORD your God am holy" (Lev 19:2), and concludes with "for you were foreigners in the land of Egypt" (Lev 19:34). For Israel, the Exodus experience became "the foundation of Israel's faith. It was the basis for knowing who Yahweh was and who they were. Yahweh was a God who delivered from oppression, and Israel was Yahweh's people."[44] This "love" for the foreigner could then involve showing the same love that they had been shown by God.[45] Since love "must be expressed in one's behaviour,"[46] this is a much greater command to obey than its counterpart in 23:9 in the Book of the Covenant, which only forbids oppression.

Leviticus 22:18–19 is a law prescribing the *inclusion* of the non-Hebrew. Chapter 22 is comprised of laws about eating sacred food (vv. 1–16), and laws governing the animals that are acceptable for sacrifice (vv. 17–33).[47] In danger of being overlooked are vv. 18–19 that address the socially marginalized. The address begins: "Any man of the house of Israel or of the aliens in Israel who presents his offering . . ." Here the foreigner that lived in Israel was invited by the Lord to "worship Yahweh as his God."[48] The resident foreigner was not only included in the social community but the worship community as well. Ensuring

43. Milgrom, *Leviticus 17–22*, 1704.

44. Malchow, *Social Justice*, 6.

45. Examples of God's love toward Israel that Israel could show to the foreigner include such things as protecting them from oppression, providing food (Exod 16:12) and water (Exod 15:25) when they had none, and visiting with them (Exod 19:18).

46. Milgrom, *Leviticus 17–22*, 1706.

47. Hartley, *Leviticus*, 352–63.

48. Ibid., 361.

the inclusion of all into the worship community regardless of ethnicity was of paramount importance to God, as evidenced by this law.

In addition to the command to be holy, Israel's past also continued to be a motivation for obeying the laws. Israel was suffering under Egyptian oppression and God acted on their behalf. Before God had offered to make a covenant with Israel, before Israel had become his covenant people, before they knew him, God was gracious to them. "I am the LORD your God who brought you out of the land of Egypt to give you the land of Canaan and to be your God" (Lev 19:36; 22:33; 23:43; 25:38, 42, 55; 26:13, 45). Further to just rescuing them, God chose to offer himself to them. Then, in a covenant relationship, God would continue to be gracious to Israel, not only by giving them the land of Canaan, but also by blessing them with his presence and with prosperity. It is not surprising, then, that the strangers/foreigners of the land, including those who may have even been considered an enemy race, were to be recipients of Israel's care and blessing. Just as God advocated for Israel before a relationship was established, Israel also was not to allow a lack of relationship to prevent them from extending the same godly care to others. Further reinforcing obedience to the laws about the socially marginalized was the command to be holy. As Israel obeyed the laws that directed them to behave with care for the foreigners in their midst, they would be obeying the command to be holy, as "justice and compassion, too, were a dimension of holiness."[49] This dimension of holiness would be manifest through *provision*, *protection*, or *inclusion* when Israel obeyed the laws. God's covenant people were to care for the strangers in their land even if they were considered enemies of Israel. As they did, they too were blessed in return by being participants in, or envoys of, God's holiness.

49. Levine, *Leviticus*, xi.

Deuteronomic Code

While the covenant made at Sinai was a historical event for these people listening to the words of Moses (Deut 1:1), it was not to remain only as such. The covenant at Sinai inaugurated the relationship between Israel and their God (Exod 19–Num 10), and its renewal in the land of Moab (Deut 1:5) would recall that event.[50] The purpose of this covenant renewal was not "because God changed, but because each generation had to recommit itself regularly in love and obedience to the Lord of the covenant."[51] While Deuteronomy is an expounding (1:5) or explaining by Moses of all that the Lord had commanded (1:3), it does more than repeat laws of the previous codes. Not only does Deuteronomy include additional laws, "but here the law is to be explained and applied by Moses to a particular situation of the Israelites."[52] Upon their entrance into the Promised Land, the law of Sinai needed to be more than a past event. For this generation hearing Moses, Deuteronomy was not only a renewal of the covenant and a reflection on Sinai, but also a renewal that prepared them for their imminent entrance into the Promised Land.

Theological Motivations

In the Deuteronomic Code the primary motivation for obedience to the laws continues to be God's historic and gracious election and redemption of undeserving Israel. The nation is continually reminded throughout the book that God made an oath with their ancestors to give them the land (1:8, 35; 6:10, 18, 23; 7:13; 8:1; 9:5; 10:11; 11:9, 21; 19:8; 26:3, 15; 27:3; 28:11; 30:20; 31:5, 20; 34:3). God chose them, not because they were deserving in any way (7:7), but because he "set his affection to love them and he chose their descendants after them, even you, above all peoples,

50. Craigie, *Deuteronomy*, 37.
51. Ibid.
52. Ibid., 92.

as it is this day" (10:15). Thus this sovereign election of God to love and make oaths with Israel should motivate a "loyalty owed by Israel in return."[53]

God's gracious act of redeeming Israel continues here to be a motivation behind the laws. When Moses recounts the Decalogue to the people he repeats God's first words spoken directly to Israel: "I am the LORD your God who brought you out of the land of Egypt, out of the house of slavery" (5:6). When God identifies himself by name, "his authority stands behind the promises or commands."[54] When he adds to this self-identity his act of freeing Israel from Egyptian oppression he "establishes the basis on which he expects them to accept his authority."[55] Thus this phrase (6:12; 8:13; 13:5, 10; 20:1; 24:17) conveys a "message of grace,"[56] reminding Israel that it was the Lord who rescued them from a life of slavery, and therefore they should respond with thankful obedience.

God's act of delivering Israel from Egypt was not only to motivate the generation of Deuteronomy but also all future generations. After directing Israel to commit themselves to God with undivided loyalty (6:1–6), Moses commands a constant awareness of God's teachings that was to be passed on to subsequent generations.

Moses directs Israel to "fear the LORD our God for our good always and for our survival, as it is today. It will be righteousness for us if we are careful to observe all these commandments before the LORD our God, just as he commanded us" (6:24–25). There is the intrinsic sense here that loving God with all one's heart is reflected by obedience that comes from the heart. The laws were not meant to be obeyed strictly out of duty to the law, but out of love for God, the law's source. This obedience subsequently prompts the blessings of God.

Thus, as with the previous law codes, the laws about the socially marginalized in Deuteronomy find their motivation in

53. Nelson, *Deuteronomy*, 10.

54. Tigay, *Deuteronomy*, 63.

55. Ibid.

56. Christensen, *Deuteronomy 1–21:9*, 114.

the Lord, the God who delivered the Israelites from Egypt and then made a covenant with them at Sinai. As at Sinai, in Moab this same Lord spoke through Moses once again, supplementing the terms of the Sinai Covenant with the laws of Deuteronomy.

As with the Book of the Covenant and the Priestly Code, the laws that involve these socially marginalized groups in Deuteronomy have a recurring theme. While the main theme of the laws about the socially marginalized in the Book of the Covenant is protection, and in the Priestly Code it is primarily inclusion, the dominant theme in the Deuteronomic Code is provision. Again, as with the previous groups of laws, themes of protection, provision, or inclusion are all present, but they have one theme that primarily serves the socially marginalized. As with the other charts, "X" represents the primary theme or function the law serves for the marginalized.

Text of Law Deuteronomy	Socially Marginalized Addressed	Primary Themes		
		Protection	Provision	Inclusion
1:16	Foreigner	X		
5:13–15	Foreigner/Slave			X
10:18–19	Foreigner/Widow/Orphan		X	
14:21	Foreigner		X	
14:29	Foreigner/Widow/Orphan		X	
15:4–11	Poor		X	
15:12–18	Slave		X	
16:9–15	Foreigner/Widow/Orphan/ Slave			X
23:15–16	Slave	X		
24:10–15	Foreigner/Poor	X		
24:17–18	Foreigner/Widow/Orphan	X		
24:19–22	Foreigner/Widow/Orphan		X	
26:11–13	Foreigner/Widow/Orphan		X	
27:19	Foreigner/Widow/Orphan	X		
28:43	Foreigner		X	
29:11	Foreigner			X
31:12	Foreigner			X

Functional Themes

With seventeen, the Deuteronomic Code has the greatest number of laws concerned with the treatment of Israel's socially marginalized population. It is the theme of provision that arises most often from these laws, almost twice as many times as the themes of protection and inclusion. While the foreigner does receive the most mention in these laws, he/she is often named alongside the widow and orphan, and rarely so with the slave and poor. There is no dominant group of people receiving attention in these laws, as they name each segment of the population, the foreigner, widow, orphan, slave, and poor, throughout. An example of each theme is provided below.

Deuteronomy 5:13–15 is an example of a law in which God's concern is inclusion of the socially marginalized. More specifically, the danger is that the working class will not be afforded a day of rest by their masters. Here in Deuteronomy 5 Moses recounts the Decalogue given to the people directly from God at Sinai. In doing so he repeats God's first words: "I am the LORD your God who brought you out of the land of Egypt, out of the house of slavery." Thus, reiterated at the outset is the motivation behind the Decalogue itself, that being the self-identity of the Lord as the God who rescued Israel from oppression and by his grace made Israel his own people.

This law of the Sabbath specifically stipulates that no one in the household, including the slave and the foreigner, is to do any work so that they "may rest as well as you" (v. 14). This law ensures that the slave and the foreigner are not forced to work every seven days out of seven by including them in the household when observing the Sabbath. "This one day a week the servant is treated as the master's equal."[57] This law concludes with the Decalogue's motivational statement repeated here: "You shall remember that you were a slave in the land of Egypt, and the LORD your God brought you out of there by a mighty hand and by an outstretched arm; therefore the LORD your God commanded you to observe the sabbath day" (v. 15).

57. Tigay, *Deuteronomy*, 69.

The law of Deut 14:29 prescribed the provision of food for the socially marginalized. The annual tithe is stipulated in vv. 22–27, followed by the tri-annual tithe in v. 28. The purpose is stated in v. 29. Within each seven-year period, on the third and sixth years, "the farmers shall not eat the tithe at the sanctuary but must deposit it in their hometowns to feed the Levites and the poor."[58] While the Levites were not socially marginalized, God had stipulated that the tithe of the land was to be used for food for the Levites (Num 18:21–24). This law in v. 29 is not meant to include the Levite with the socially marginalized but rather "to put the annual tithe in that year to a different use."[59] Thus the law here would seem to expand on the law in Numbers 18, to include the local foreigner, orphan, and widow as recipients of the tithe. The purpose was that the socially marginalized "within one's town"[60] could "eat and be satisfied" (14:29).[61]

As the landowning farmers blessed the poor with the tithe of food from their harvest, the Lord in turn would bless the farmers in all their work. Thus, out of a desire for a good harvest for themselves, the farmers would be motivated to give this tithe. Through this "circle of generosity empowered by blessing"[62] those who were self-sufficient supported those who were not. Thus, both groups were "enabled to learn and understand their continual dependence upon God."[63]

While Deut 24:19–22 carries the practical theme of provision, it is also another law directed at the farmers as the ones responsible for making such provision. This law primarily makes provision of food for the poor, but in doing so protects against starvation. The appeal to Israel to behave compassionately because

58. Christensen, *Deuteronomy 1–21:9*, 144.

59. Mayes, *Deuteronomy*, 246.

60. Christensen, *Deuteronomy 1–21:9*, 305.

61. This suggests that the food was either "stored for subsequent distribution when need arose, or else distributed immediately to the needy persons" (Craigie, *Deuteronomy*, 234).

62. Nelson, *Deuteronomy*, 191.

63. Craigie, *Deuteronomy*, 234.

of their experience as slaves in Egypt is also the motivation for this law of the harvest (v. 22), in addition to the motive of God's blessing (v. 19). Like the laws in the Holiness Code (Lev 19:9–10; 23:22), this law forbids a farmer from going over the harvest field a second time. What was missed the first time was to be left in the field for the poor, named here as the foreigner, the orphan, and the widow. "The spirit of this legislation expresses clearly the awareness that was to exist within the covenant community for all classes of people."[64] This law not only provided food for the poor, but also protected their dignity as well. Rather than having to beg for food the poor were provided the opportunity to work for their own food like the farmer.[65] Such behavior by the farmer was not just an act of charity but also an expression of thankfulness to God for the harvest.[66]

If there is one text that best summarizes these themes it is Deut 15:4–11. The law of this text is directed toward those in Israelite society who are self-sufficient. "They are shown to have not only the capacity to affect the shape of social reality but also the capacity to bring upon the whole of society either curse or blessing."[67] This depends on how they act toward the poor.

There are a total of six emphatic uses of the infinitive absolute in vv. 4–11. All of them are related to *emphatic* giving to the poor that will result in God's *emphatic* blessing. In this text, God's blessing to make the nation of Israel prosperous is directly dependant upon their obedience to God's command to *abundantly* lend to the poor, thereby making provision for them.

The text is framed by the phrases "There will be no poor among you" (v. 4), and "For a poor one will not stop from the midst of the land" (v. 11). The sense of the text is that if Israel obeyed the laws concerning the poor, they would be so blessed by God that poverty would be abolished. But this was not to be the case, as indicated by v. 11. Perhaps that is why, when relating to the poor, Israel was warned against hard-heartedness

64. Ibid. 310.
65. Ibid.
66. Ibid.
67. Hamilton, *Social Justice*, 15.

(v. 7), a wicked heart (v. 9), and an evil heart (v. 10). Giving to the poor was not to be done grudgingly or dutifully, but from a generous heart. This may also be reflected by the "emphatic" giving encouraged throughout the text.

If the laws about the poor were to be obeyed only out of duty, the emphatic uses would not have been necessary; but perhaps it is obedience from the heart that God is encouraging through the emphatic uses. People can open their hands to the poor and lend, but if it is from the heart then the result is a hand that "*greatly* opens" and "*abundantly* lends" (v. 8). The same senses are repeated in vv. 10–11. Rather than requiring giving from an open hand, God again requires that Israel "*abundantly* give" and "*greatly* open your hand" (vv. 10–11). If that were the case then God would not only bless, but "*abundantly* bless" (v. 4). The text of Deut 15:4–11 best summarizes the laws about the socially marginalized in Deuteronomy, and perhaps the Torah as well.

The look back to God's liberation of Israel from Egyptian slavery continues to be a primary motivation to obey the laws here in Deuteronomy. This look back was a necessary reminder of God's advocacy on their behalf, in order to encourage this new generation of Israel for the challenges that faced them as they were about to enter the Promised Land. It is quite practical that at this time provision is the theme that arises most in the laws about the socially marginalized in Deuteronomy, and the foreigner, and then widow and orphan, are those most named. As Israel goes into the land to conquer those who are foreigners to them, their enemies, God stipulates that Israel treat those who survive and continue to dwell in the land with care. Emphasizing provision for the widows and orphans through their repeated mention is also timely as Israel, about to go to war, will lose many husbands and fathers.

Summary

God has chosen to reveal himself to humanity in a variety of ways. Apart from direct experience of God, perhaps the most prominent mode of God's self revelation is his written word.

Turn to any book in the Bible and some facet of God's character is revealed. This study has turned to the laws in the Torah concerning Israel's most vulnerable population, and there the compassion of God is revealed.

The socially marginalized in Israelite society included all those who were not part of the typical landowning familial social structure that sustained and secured a person's life necessities. In the laws they are the widow, orphan, foreigner, slave, and the poor. Throughout these laws Israel is given specific stipulations regarding how they ought to care for the socially marginalized. They range primarily from providing them food and clothing, to protecting them from being abused or exploited, to ensuring that their plight did not exclude them from the social or religious community.

Thus, as the charts in each section outline, the primary focus of all the laws concerning these disenfranchised members of the community can be summarized according to the three primary themes that arise from each law. Each law primarily served the socially marginalized group or groups it addressed by directing Israel to *provide for*, *protect*, or *include* them. Not only are these themes reflective of God's character in the law, but they are reflected in his actions as well. When God delivered Israel from Egypt he *protected* them from further harm (Exod 3:7–9; 7:1–5; 12:33–41), he *provided* them with food as they traveled towards the Promised Land (Exod 16:12–21; 17:1–7), and he *included* them unto himself in a covenantal relationship (Exod 19–24). Thus, those in covenant relationship with the Lord were expected to behave likewise toward the socially marginalized and, therefore, vulnerable in their midst.

Throughout the Torah, God is presented as the source of these laws and therefore, not only do the laws reflect his character, but they also carry his authority. God introduced the laws given at Sinai saying, "I am the LORD your God, who brought you out of the land of Egypt, out of the house of slavery." By this, future generations of Israel came to know that it was the Lord who delivered them from their Egyptian bondage. As an act of grace God chose to rescue undeserving Israel and enter into a covenant relationship with them. Israel was told to "remember that you were a slave in Egypt" (Deut 26:12), and obey because "the LORD your God redeemed you from there; therefore I am commanding you to do this thing" (Deut 24:18, 22). They are told to "be holy, for I the LORD your God am holy" (Lev 19:1; 20:7, 26; 21:5). Obedience to the laws would enable them to reflect God's character. Among those laws were the laws that addressed the socially marginalized, and therefore vulnerable, population within Israel.

Beyond the Old Testament: Christian Understanding

From the heart of these laws about the socially marginalized arise these themes of protection, provision, and inclusion. While the twenty-first century Christian may find little relevance in a specific law, understanding that these themes reveal the compassion and nature of God's character may provide a way towards understanding their specific relevance to us. While Christians are not Israelites, they are in covenant relationship with the same God who has revealed himself as compassionate when he rescued Israel from Egypt. He is the same God who prescribed laws motivating his covenant people to protect, provide for, and include those who needed to be protected and provided for, and were in danger of being isolated from mainstream society or from community of worship. While Christians are not bound to these laws, they are bound to the God of those laws through a different covenant, and as such, they too ought to show forth the characteristics of their God.

The Exodus event clearly demonstrated the love that God had for Israel and the extent to which he would involve himself in human affairs in order to show them that love. The Christian however, looks back to an event when that same God once again involved himself in human affairs in order to show the love he has, not only for his people, but for all people. In both cases, God's love was made known through his practical actions on behalf of those under oppression. For the Israelites it was release from Egyptian oppression and for the Christian it is release from the oppression of sin. Again, in both cases, God blesses his covenant people by working through them in order to continue to bring about his advocacy for the oppressed through their practical actions of protecting, providing, and including those marginalized people in their society.

For Christians, holiness is imparted to them upon entering into covenant relationship with God. They too, however, must choose to align their behavior with their covenant status. As they show forth the compassion of God through the practical means of protecting, providing for, or including those marginalized people in their society, as the law directed Israel to do, Christians will be participating in God's godliness or holiness. Again, Christians, as the Israelites were, are motivated to behave as their God would by remembering their God's past redeeming actions on their behalf.

Being God's people comes with the obligation of behaving in a "godly" way. This was accomplished by the Israelites through obedience to the laws, which would result in the compassionate treatment of Israel's socially marginalized population. In the culture in which the Christian exists today, godly behavior continues to be seen wherever compassionate treatment toward a socially marginalized person is extended. This godly compassion toward the poor is best demonstrated, not just by protecting, providing, or including the socially marginalized, but by doing these things extravagantly so. Since Christians have personally experienced the abundant compassion of God when he liberated them from sin and death to life, they too, as Israel was, are in a position to further extend that godly compassion to others.

Just as Israel was motivated to be godly by God's gracious act of redeeming them from Egyptian bondage, Christians can also look back in their own personal history and recount the undeserved redemption that God graciously afforded them. God has *protected* Christians from eternal death and slavery to sin and *provided* them with fullness of life (temporal and eternal) and *included* them in the community of God as he has bound them to himself in a covenantal relationship through Jesus.

New Testament Applications

It is the life of Jesus that Christians often turn to when determining what godly living looks like, and there see how he protected, provided for, and included those at risk in his environment in practical ways. But Christians often fail to appreciate the significance of Jesus' words when he refers to the law: "Do not think that I came to abolish the Law or the Prophets; I did not come to abolish but to fulfill. For truly I say to you, until heaven and earth pass away, not the smallest letter or stroke shall pass from the Law until all is accomplished" (Matt 5:17–18). Heaven and earth have not passed away and, therefore, neither has the law. Since the law is not abolished in Christ but fulfilled in Christ, to have a better understanding of the law is to have a better understanding of Jesus.

Through the works of Jesus the law is completed, but not nullified. Through the fulfillment of the law Jesus opened the way for a new covenant. God spoke of this new covenant through the prophet Jeremiah saying,

> Behold, days are coming when I will make a new covenant with the house of Israel and with the house of Judah, not like the covenant which I made with their fathers in the day I took them by the hand to bring them out of the land of Egypt, my covenant which they broke, although I was a husband to them. But this is the covenant which I will make with the house of Israel after those days: I will put my law within them and on their heart I will write it; and I will be their God, and they shall be my people (Jer 31:31–33).

The law exists today in the heart of those with whom God has established this new covenant through Jesus. The law of God that was external and stipulated that compassionate things must be done for others is now internally written on the heart of Christians. God's desire for the advocacy of the socially marginalized has become the internal desires of his covenant people as well.

When Jesus was asked to name the greatest commandment in the law he answered, "'You shall love the Lord your God with all your heart, and with all your soul, and with all your mind.'

This is the great and foremost commandment. The second is like it, 'You shall love your neighbor as yourself'" (Matt 22:37–39). Neither of these laws is a New Testament idea. They are found first in the Torah: love of God in Deut 6:5 and love of neighbor in Lev 19:18. Jesus intended that these two laws be understood as intrinsically connected. This is how the apostle John understood them:

> If someone says, "I love God," and hates his brother, he is a liar; for the one who does not love his brother whom he has seen, cannot love God whom he has not seen. And this commandment we have from him, that the one who loves God should love his brother also" (1 John 4:20–21).

To express one's love for a neighbor through practical helpful ways is to express to that person, not only the love of God, but one's love for God as well.

Jesus then emphasized further the command, "You shall love your neighbor as yourself" (Lev 19:18). He paraphrased the command by saying, "treat people the same way you want them to treat you" and then added, "for this is the Law and the Prophets" (Matt 7:12). Jesus equates the law with showing love to one's neighbor.

This command to love one's neighbor, first found in the Torah and witnessed in the life of Jesus, also continues beyond the Gospels. As the church grew, the Greek-speaking Christians complained that the widows among them were not receiving "the daily serving of food" (Acts 6:1). In order to ensure they were no longer neglected, the early church restructured itself, adding the office of the deacon.

Such service to those who were vulnerable was to be the hallmark of a person who was truly religious. "Pure and undefiled religion in the sight of our God and Father is this: to visit orphans and widows in their distress" (Jas 1:27). James also equated the law with love of neighbor saying, "If, however, you are fulfilling the royal law according to the Scripture, 'You shall love your neighbor as yourself,' you are doing well" (Jas 2:8).

On behalf of the poor, Paul urged the Corinthian Christians to set aside money on a weekly basis so when he came to them it would be ready for him to collect (1 Cor 16:2). Later (2 Cor 8:15) Paul drew on Exod 16:18, reminding them that just as God provided food for Moses and Israel in the desert, they too could trust God to provide for them and therefore could give to the poor without fear. Paul too equates love of neighbor with the law. To the Galatians Christians he says, "For all the law is fulfilled in one word, even in this: You shall love your neighbor as yourself" (Gal 5:14). And then to the Christians in Rome he says,

> he who loves his neighbor has fulfilled the law. For this, "You shall not commit adultery, You shall not murder, You shall not steal, You shall not covet," and if there is any other commandment, it is summed up in this saying, "You shall love your neighbor as yourself." Love does no wrong to a neighbor; therefore love is the fulfillment of the law (Rom 13:8–10).

From the Gospels to Acts to the Epistles, expressing love to a neighbor finds its roots in the Torah. To live according to the law "Love your neighbor as yourself" is to live according to the Torah.

A Contemporary Application

Among those in greatest need of this love manifested through practical compassion are people with developmental disabilities. Regardless of family status, religion, or ethnicity, people with developmental disabilities across the world have a history of being marginalized by mainstream society to such a degree that their very lives are at risk. "In darker times of human civilization, such as the city-states of ancient Greece or Hitler's Nazi Germany, thousands and millions of people with some kind of disabling condition were killed in the belief that wiping out everyone with a specific disabled 'gene,' (the eugenic movement) would prevent future malformations in the human race."[68] Treating any group of people this way today violates Article 16 of the *Universal Declaration of Human Rights* as adopted and

68. Webb-Mitchell, *Unexpected Guests*, 50.

proclaimed by the General Assembly of the United Nations on December 10, 1948. Yet, even today, the argument is being made that human rights do not apply to some people because they are not fully human persons. This approach that ethicists such as Princeton's Peter Singer are taking today is called the *actuality principle*. This approach seeks to define human personhood as requiring a "developed capacity for conscious self-reflective intelligence."[69] Peter Singer questions the humanity of a person who has a severe intellectual disability when he says: "Infanticide (the killing of infants) should be permitted whenever it is clear that the baby will never function as a 'full' human being."[70] In other words, if a person does not have the required intellect to qualify as 'truly being human', then not only should that person's human rights be revoked but that person's right to life as well.

Regardless of people's developmental disabilities, and the degree to which a given society has, and will, marginalize this people group, they are the target of physical aggression, of being despised and treated as less than human, and of being isolated and neglected. In some cultures, people with disabilities are seen as a nuisance or drain on the economy, while in others they are despised as a curse or are subjected to abandonment and infanticide.

Fortunately there are those who recognize the intrinsic value of every person, and focus their resources toward ensuring that people with developmental disabilities are afforded the same rights, respect, and life opportunities that most take for granted.

What might obedience to God's laws about treatment of this group of marginalized people look like today? A practical example is the ministry of Christian Horizons.[71] Regardless of their abilities, status, religion, or race, all people who are served

69. Stassen and Gushee, *Kingdom Ethics*, 221–22.

70. Thomas, "Deadly Compassion," 14–21.

71. Loney, "Together We Are Stronger," 4. Christian Horizons was founded in 1965 by Jim and Adrienne Reese, who were discontented with services available to help them with their son who has a developmental disability. Christian Horizons is currently the largest provider of services to people with these exceptional needs in Ontario.

in Christian Horizons, are *protected* from the various forms of abuse people with developmental disabilities often suffer, be they physical, sexual, emotional, financial, or relational. Christian Horizons also ensures that the supports are *provided* on an individual basis rather than on the older institutional model. In addition to such things as dignity, respect, and love, Christian Horizons also provides the freedom of choice, honoring the will of the individual. This support of individual choice ensures that each person's preferences, from choice of religion and place of worship to the choice of meals, room color, and daily schedule are provided. *Inclusion* in one's community is probably the greatest challenge that people with developmental disabilities face. From job and career opportunities, to places of worship, to extra-curricular school activities, to making friends, Christian Horizons strives to fully integrate a person into the community in which they live, advocating to overcome and remove the prejudicial barriers present in mainstream society that have prevented such inclusion.

In the twenty-first century, the need for practical compassion, which manifests itself through means of protecting, providing for and including the vulnerable in a society, is as pressing as ever. Among those most vulnerable are children, people with developmental disabilities, and single parent families, found both locally and globally. Without good advocacy on their behalf, fullness of life is not only difficult, but in many cases will cease altogether. The poverty stricken and vulnerable will always be a part of local and global societies (Matt 26:11; Mark 14:7; John 12:8) and therefore provide anyone seeking to walk in the ways of the Lord endless opportunities to be an expression of God's godly compassion. This is not just a compassion that is felt in the heart, but is worked out practically through the protection, provision for, and inclusion of society's vulnerable and socially marginalized peoples.

Bibliography

Balentine, Samuel E. *Leviticus.* Interpretation. Louisville, KY: Westminster John Knox Press, 2002.

Brown, Francis, et al. *The Brown-Driver-Briggs Hebrew and English Lexicon.* Peabody, MA: Hendrickson, 2000.

Christensen, Duane, L. *Deuteronomy 1–21:9.* WBC. Nashville: Thomas Nelson, 2001.

Craigie, Peter C. *Deuteronomy.* NICOT. Grand Rapids: Eerdmans, 1976.

de Vaux, Roland. *Ancient Israel: Social Institutions.* New York: McGraw-Hill, 1965.

Dumbrell, William J. *Covenant and Creation.* Flemington Markets, NSW, Australia: Lancer Books, 1984.

Fretheim, Terence E. *God and World in the Old Testament.* Nashville: Abingdon, 2005.

Hamilton, Jeffries M. *Social Justice and Deuteronomy.* Atlanta: Scholars Press, 1992.

Hartley, John E. *Leviticus.* WBC. Waco, TX: Word Books, 1992.

Janzen, Waldemar. *Old Testament Ethics: A Paradigmatic Approach.* Louisville, KY: John Knox Press, 1993.

Knohl, Israel. *The Sanctuary of Silence.* Minneapolis: Fortress Press, 1995.

Lee, Won W. *Punishment and Forgiveness in Israel's Migratory Campaign.* Grand Rapids: Eerdmans, 2003.

Levine, Baruch A. *Leviticus.* JPS Torah Commentary. New York: Jewish Publication Society, 1989.

Loney, Grace. "Together We Are Stronger." *Exceptional Possibilities* (Spring 2007) 4.

Malchow, Bruce V. "Social Justice in the Israelite Law Codes." *WW* 4 (1984) 299–306.

———. *Social Justice in the Hebrew Bible.* Collegeville, MN: Liturgical Press, 1996.

Matthews, Victor H., and Don C. Benjamin. *Social World of Ancient Israel 1250–587 BCE.* Peabody, MA: Hendrickson, 1993.

Mayes, A. D. H. *Deuteronomy.* NCB. London: Oliphants, 1979.

McNutt, Paula. *Reconstructing the Society of Ancient Israel.* Louisville, KY: Westminster John Knox Press, 1999.

Milgrom, Jacob. *Leviticus 1–16.* AB. New York: Doubleday, 1991.

———. *Leviticus 17–22.* AB. New York: Doubleday, 2000.

Nelson, Richard D. *Deuteronomy.* OTL. Louisville KY: Westminster John Knox Press, 2002.

North, Robert. *Sociology of the Biblical Jubilee.* Rome: Pontifical Biblical Institute, 1954.

Patrick, Dale. *Old Testament Law.* Atlanta: John Knox Press, 1985.

Perdue, Leo G. "The Israelite and Early Jewish Family." In *Families in Ancient Israel,* by Leo G. Perdue, Joseph Blenkinsopp, John J. Collins, and Carol L. Meyers, 163–222. Louisville, KY: Westminster John Knox Press, 1997.

Sprinkle, Joe M. *The Book of the Covenant: A Literary Approach.* JSOTSup 174. London: T&T Clark, 1994.

Stassen, Glen H. and David P. Gushee. *Kingdom Ethics*. Downers Grove, IL: InterVarsity Press, 2003.

Thomas, Gary L. "Deadly Compassion." *CT* (16 June 1997) 14–21.

Tigay, Jeffrey H. *Deuteronomy*. JPS Torah Commentary. Philadelphia: Jewish Publication Society, 1996.

Webb-Mitchell, Brett. *Unexpected Guests at God's Banquet.* New York: Crossroad, 1994.

Wenham, Gordon J. *Leviticus.* NICOT. Grand Rapids: Eerdmans, 1979.

[*MJTM* 10 (2008–2009) 140–73]

Go Up and Possess the Garden of the World: The Ontario Baptist Mission to the North West Territories, 1869–1870

James Tyler Robertson
McMaster Divinity College, Hamilton, ON

As the *Canadian Baptist Register*[1] reviewed the events that shaped its denomination throughout 1869, several pages were consumed discussing Canada's newly acquired North West Territories, with a special concentration on the fact that there was no Baptist presence within the region.[2] In order to correct this, missionaries were dispatched to gather information and report back to Ontario Baptists so that plans for western expansion could get underway as soon as was feasible. Money was raised and the *Canadian Baptist* newspaper offered numerous reports to its readership to inspire people to uproot and make their claims in the burgeoning land beyond the horizon. No longer was Rupert's Land destined to be a howling wilderness occupied only by natives and fur traders; the west was to be opened up to the influence of Canadians, and, as was argued in the denominational literature, to the influence of the Baptist Church. However, it would not be until 1873 that the first residential Baptist missionary to the area would arrive[3] and while some have argued that this gap in time from conception to realization was due to the limited vision of the Ontario Missionary Societies or a lack

1. The *Canadian Baptist Register* is also referred to in this article simply as the *Register*. Likewise, the *Canadian Baptist* is sometimes referred to as the *Baptist*.

2. It must be noted that the articles pertaining to the North West Territories occur in the *Canadian Baptist Register* of 1870 as that was the edition that dealt with the events of the previous year.

3. This was Alexander MacDonald, who would earn the moniker "Pioneer" for his undertaking of this assignment.

of financial support from the more established churches in Ontario,[4] it is possible that a large portion of the problem lay not in Ontario but in the North West Territories themselves.

In its own words the *Register* stated, "the North West Territories present one of the strangest, if not one of the most complex compounds, in the early history of any country."[5] Comments like these were inspired by the insurrection that occurred in Red River after the sale of the Territories by the Hudson's Bay Company to the newly formed Dominion of Canada in 1869. Members of the Métis population set up their own Provisional Government in defiance of both the H.B.C. and Canada.[6] Later on, Fenians from the United States launched an assault on the Territory in an effort to thwart British interests north of the border. Given that the Ontario Home Mission Board tried to "sell" the idea of colonizing the Territories as something of a golden opportunity, such tumult as occurred in the region had more potential to derail the calling to head west than anything else. While it would be unrealistic not to include the aforementioned reasons for the Baptists' delay in getting to the west, it is worth investigating the *Canadian Baptist*, the *Canadian Baptist Register*, correspondence dating from the time, newspapers, journals, and the work of other historians to see how the violence in the Red River area impacted the Baptist mission to the west.

In order to understand how the Baptists wanted to inspire their people to move, it is essential to understand something of the men who were sent to accomplish this assignment.

4. Grant, *Church*, 50, says, "Despite this vigorous beginning, the Baptists were hampered for many years by their failure to secure a solid base of eastern support."

5. Davidson and Baldwin, "Report of the Deputation of the North West Territories," *Canadian Baptist Register*, 1870, 48.

6. For more on the Red River Rebellion, see Berger, *Sense of Power*, 56–59; Bumsted, *Red River Rebellion*; Messamore, *Canada's Governor General*, 186–89; Stacey, *Canada*, 17. For the role of the churches in the Red River struggle see Coutts, *Road to the Rapids*, 88, 107–9, 170; Grant, *Church*, 31–32; Semple, *Dominion*, 174–77, 292, 414.

Missionaries[7] Rev. Dr. Thomas Davidson and Rev. Thomas Baldwin[8] were both born in Ontario—Davidson in Perth and Baldwin near Hamilton—and both were considered successful pastors at their respective churches, also located in Ontario. Davidson had been friends with R. A. Fyfe[9] since the two first met at Montreal Theological College; he had been the secretary of the Home Mission Convention for fifteen years and seemed a natural selection for the mission at hand. Baldwin was less prominent but equally equipped for the task. He had successfully pastored churches in East Oxford and Ingersoll, and was referred to in the *Register* as "the Missionary" every year after his expedition to the west.[10] In their own words the two men wrote their intention in taking on this calling:

> [We want] to go and explore the country known as the Great North West Territories, and report to you upon its physical, political and religious condition. That, with correct knowledge of the country, in its soil and climate, the Baptists might judge of the probable future of that country, and better understand their duties, as a body of Christians, towards that vast Territory, which has now become a part of the Dominion of Canada.[11]

These two men were chosen because they understood the mind of the average Baptist in Ontario and they were to view the west through those Ontario Baptist eyes and bring back reports that would entice the people they were called to represent.

Throughout 1869, Davidson and Baldwin explored the area around Red River and wrote numerous reports back to the

7. ". . . up to the present moment the North-West territory is as much a foreign country as British India," wrote A. T. Wood, "Red River Deputation," *Canadian Baptist,* 27 January 1870, 2.

8. For more in-depth information on the two men, see McLaurin, *Pioneering in Western Canada*, 41.

9. Fyfe was arguably the most prominent champion of the cause of western expansion.

10. Hoyes, "Thomas Baldwin—St. Thomas," *Canadian Baptist Register*, October 1872, 31.

11. Davidson and Baldwin, "Report of the Deputation to the North West Territories," *Canadian Baptist Register*, 1870, 45.

Ontario Baptists encouraging the denomination to spread its influence westward.[12] The arguments used to inspire Baptist emigration were threefold: the love of Christ[13] and the desire to share his gospel, the love of country and the desire to increase the prestige of the Dominion of Canada for its citizens and its Monarch, and the fertility of the land being described.[14] The Baptists were encouraged to "Go up and possess the land"[15] that lay out before them.[16] Statements like this brought to mind

12. Boulton, *Reminiscenses*, 41, says that most inhabitants of Ontario knew very little about the North West Territory. He writes, "[The North West Territories were] isolated from Canada, little was known to the Canadian people of the vast resources of the Hudson's Bay region."

13. It appears that the love of Christ was what Davidson's own church (Aylmer) cited as the primary reason for his acceptance of the assignment. In the Aylmer Church Annual Report of 9 May, 1869 the following is recorded: "Considering the interest of the Gospel of Christ in the Regular Baptist Denomination by the action of the Missionary Board at their last meeting in appointing Dr. Davidson our pastor to explore the Red River Country and represent the interest of the Denomination. Therefore we the church of Malahide and Aylmer willingly assent to his accepting the appointment." It is interesting to note, in light of the following footnote, that land was not the central issue for the church. Although the *Canadian Baptist Register* gave the quality of the land the lion's share of the attention, Aylmer church believed it was the duty of their pastor to serve the Gospel of Christ. This does bring up an interesting point regarding how much influence denominational literature impacted/represented the average Baptist. However, it is also very possible that Aylmer had no concept of the land quality prior to Davidson's report and therefore would have had no reason to mention it.

14. It is worth noting that this is the order present in the *Canadian Baptist*. However, within the pages of the *Canadian Baptist Register* the issue of land is central and makes up the majority of the information dedicated to the subject at hand.

15. "[E]ach interposing event of Providence reiterates the command to our people, 'Go up and possess the land'" (Davidson, "Lecture on the North-West," *Canadian Baptist,* 21 October 1869, 2).

16. Davidson and Baldwin both exhibited deep respect for the land. They believed that the ground needed to be tilled and that the Native population was not willing to pay the money or do the work to improve the land. They wrote: "They have no taxes to pay, no public improvements to do . . . and the half-breeds are satisfied . . . with the present state of things" (Davidson and Baldwin, "Report of the Deputation of the North West Territories," *Canadian Baptist Register*, 1870, 48). However, one could easily make the argument that

Scripture references to the time when God issued a similar command to the Israelites before their entrance into the Promised Land. Such allusions to Scripture revealed a national ideology, within Baptist ranks at least, that proposed that Canada was to be a nation dedicated to the service of God. The missionaries used such biblical incentives to encourage their fellow Baptists to head west and insure that their presence was felt. The "Promised Land" of the west was also frequently reported as being incredibly lush and fertile (a land of milk and honey, so to speak) and was said to be the key to personal and national prosperity. The possession of those natural resources could only bring prestige and wealth to the people and it was stated that the North West was the "Garden of the world and the path to empire."[17]

In keeping with the idea of Canada as a nation reserved for God, many articles lamented the severe lack of faithful Christianity in the Red River community. This was not due to a shortage of ecclesiastical institutions, because the region was already heavily populated with Roman Catholics, Anglicans, Presbyterians, and Methodists.[18] Despite the presence of these Christian bodies, Davidson made the following comment regarding the

the Native population was happy with the land and that Davidson and Baldwin's ideas were the ones in need of being corrected.

17. "In my next I shall speak of the advantages of the North-West as a country, which has been described as 'the path to empire and the garden of the world'" (Davidson, "The Great North-West," *Canadian Baptist*, 2 September 1869, 2).

18. "[The Anglicans] have, to a certain extent, been successful in gaining a healthful, religious influence over the half-breeds, and in educating them in their parochial schools, which is the only system of education existing in the country . . . The Presbyterians have about 800 members and adherents, under the pastoral care of the Rev. Mr. Black and Rev. Mr. Fletcher" (Davidson and Baldwin, "Report of the Deputation of the North West Territories," *Canadian Baptist Register*, 1870, 49). Another article discussed the fact that there were two Wesleyan Methodists and that while there was no word about Methodist Societies starting there was a parsonage being built and a chapel being erected. The author then went on to state that the Anglican Church was, "more numerous than those of the Catholic Church or any other" (Davidson, "The North-West Territories," *Canadian Baptist*, 26 August 1869, 2).

spiritual state of the land: "[T]he people have abundance of religious means, considering their number; but true vital godliness is at a low ebb."[19] He encouraged his readers to remedy that situation and referenced them back to one of his previous articles that linked the lack of spirituality to the lack of Baptists in the region. In that article Davidson reported: "At present there are no Baptists in Red River or westward."[20]

Such an array of Christian denominations already present in the region begs the question: why were the Baptists so far behind the other churches? Historians of the period are almost unanimous in the appraisal that the delayed arrival of Baptists in the Western Frontier was due largely to their church governance in Ontario. It can be said that any Christian denomination's strength is also usually its weakness and that appears to be the case with the Baptist missions in the nineteenth century. The individual autonomy of each church gave the Baptist ecclesiology an appealing freedom but the lack of an overarching leadership structure made combined initiatives more difficult to realize. Each church struggled just to maintain itself in the largely frontier world of Ontario, which made it hard to fathom raising money and sending people into the far west. Harry Renfree comments that it was precisely the lack of Baptist unity that impacted their mission to the west. He writes, "Why were the Baptists so late on the scene? The lack of unity in central Canada was one critical factor. While two missionary societies had

19. Davidson, "The Great North-West," *Canadian Baptist*, 2 September 1869, 2.

20. Davidson, "To the North West and Back," *Canadian Baptist*, 19 August 1869, 2. Despite their condemnations of the Red River faith communities, both men recorded their deep appreciation for the friendly disposition of the other Protestants in so isolated a region. They wrote: "The Venerable Archdeacon McLean, and others of that clergy, showed us much brotherly and Christian kindness, which in that far off land, we felt as coming from God's own servants" (Davidson, "To the North West and Back," *Canadian Baptist*, 19 August 1869, 49). Another example: "Episcopal clergymen called on us to-day and were both courteous and communicative, bidding us God speed in our mission" (Davidson and Baldwin, "The Great North West," *Canadian Baptist*, 12 August 1869, 2). However, the aforementioned kindness did not eliminate the drive in Davidson and Baldwin to bring the Baptist perspective to the area.

developed, their focus was on missions within their own region."[21] Baptist historian C. C. McLaurin would have agreed with this statement as well. In his extensive volume dedicated solely to Baptist work in Western Canada he wrote:

> The Ontario Home Missions Convention, according to its charter, was confined in its missionary work to the Province of Ontario. Authorities were compelled to organize the Foreign Missionary Society of Ontario in order to send Rev. A. V. Timpay and J. McLaurin to India, but it did not seem possible to organize another Society to send a Missionary to the North West. I suppose it looked too insignificant a mission field to require a Society, and no organization of Baptists in Canada could, according to its Charter, assume any responsibility for work in the great, lone land.[22]

The churches with strong, centralized government like the Anglicans, Presbyterians, and Catholics were able to see the need to spread to the West and mobilize rapidly so that by the late nineteenth century, when the Baptists finally arrived, some of the other denominations had been there for over thirty years.[23]

21. Renfree, *Heritage and Horizon*, 171–72.

22. McLaurin, *Pioneering in Western Canada*, 31–32.

23. Lord Selkirk began filling Red River with Scottish settlers from 1811 to 1815 in an attempt to build a predominantly Scottish settlement. While there were, no doubt, some clergy in attendance even then, for the purpose of this paper this note will concentrate more on when the churches were considered officially founded. For more on the nuanced story of the founding of Red River see Campey, *The Silver Chief*, ch. 7. The Anglican Church: "Founded in 1829, St. Andrew's [Anglican] was one of the prominent and most populous communities in nineteenth-century Red River," says Coutts, *Road to the Rapids*, xii. 1845 saw the arrival of A. A. Tache, and in 1851 he was appointed coadjutor bishop of the area. Tache enjoyed profound popularity with the Métis (including Louis Riel, upon whom he had quite an impact). Presbyterian John Black had arrived in 1851 (he also hosted Davidson and Baldwin in his church, allowing them to preach. This is referenced in a subsequent section of the paper). While the Methodists had been at work to the north and west of the Red River settlement they did not officially appoint a minister to the region until 1868, a Toronto man by the name of George Young. For a concise summary of this see Grant, *Church*, 30–33. These statistics strengthen Renfree's statement: "Other denominations were already well established [in Red River]" (Renfree, *Heritage and Horizon*, 168.

Baldwin and Davidson were aware that this unspiritual atmosphere or "churchianity"[24] as they called it, of the frontier could be seen as a deterrent, and not an incentive, to many Baptists. Without Baptist institutions supporting Baptist theology in the area, the likelihood that members of the denomination would move there was minimal. The *Canadian Baptist* printed this comment:

> Baptists have had no encouragement to go and make their homes in the land. They know if they did, they would leave the means of grace which they so highly prize for themselves and leave their children behind them; and parents should be slow to remove with their children into a country where there are none of the means of grace such as their own views of the truth could approve.[25]

Therefore the men concluded that a two-fold approach was needed. First, the denomination needed to send a missionary who would be willing to stay and build the necessary structures to support Baptist culture in the region.[26] They wrote:

> We would not recommend the Convention to send a missionary for the sake of the present inhabitants, but for the purpose of having a man of energy and pastoral experience on the ground, to secure building sites in the rising towns, which must immediately spring up with the rapid increase of population; and with the higher purpose still of gathering people for the future cause and for the glory of God.[27]

Next, those interested in moving should attempt to move out in communities to ease the transition and bring a more stable

24. "There is more churchianity than christianity [sic]" wrote Davidson, "The Great North-West," *Canadian Baptist*, 2 September 1869, 2.

25. Davidson and Baldwin, "Report of the Deputation of the North West Territories," *Canadian Baptist Register*, 1870, 49.

26. Davidson and Baldwin frequently referred to the loneliness of the prairies and even reported that the arrival of the *Canadian Baptist* did much to ease their homesickness. They wrote: "[A *Canadian Baptist*] dated June 17th, came last night, and was eagerly read" (Davidson, "Our Journey to Red River," *Canadian Baptist,* 22 July 1869, 2).

27. Davidson and Baldwin, "Report of the Deputation of the North West Territories," *Canadian Baptist Register*, 1870, 50.

Baptist presence.[28] Davidson made this comment: "I should say the best plan would be for Canadians to move in colonies . . . They would then have congenial society and soon a church and chapel of their own, and a Pastor."[29] If these two events could take place, it was argued, then the Ontario Baptists could take their rightful place alongside the other denominations in the struggle to save souls in the new frontier.[30]

However, it was not simply the salvation of souls that was used to draw Baptists to the new land. As has already been stated, the purchase of the North West was also seen as a tremendous blessing for the young nation of Canada. With such incalculable resources available for the general public, the promise of wealth and prestige was a powerful persuader. Coupled with that was the pride at being able to expand the Dominion of Canada and the might of the British crown. The following report from Davidson in the early days of their journey is an example of the profound and moving impact both nationalism and imperialism had on the people of the time:

> It was a pleasant relief to us when we came two miles north of Pembina, to the International Boundary line . . . On the South side are the letters "U.S." and on the North side "H.B. Co." Bro. Baldwin

28. He did assure his readers that there were other Canadians in Red River who were examining the place for themselves. He wrote: "We have met a goodly number of Canadians since coming here, some of them settlers, and others tourists, who have come to see the country and settle if they like" (Davidson, "Our Journey to Red River," *Canadian Baptist*, 22 July 1869, 2).

29. Davidson, "To the North West and Back," *Canadian Baptist*, 19 August 1869, 2.

30. A point of interest that cannot be pursued due to the focus of this paper is the burgeoning movement for the trans-Canada railway that was going on at that time. Although it was mentioned only a few times in the *Canadian Baptist*, Davidson recognized that the railway was the only way Canada could hope to truly colonize the west. He wrote: "a good railroad through British territory [is] the only proper and efficient means of colonizing the Red River country, and the immense valley of the Sascatchewan [sic] beyond, with a people British in feeling and ideas, and who will cherish their connection with Canada, and foster commercial relations with our people" (Davidson, "To the North West and Back," *Canadian Baptist*, 19 August 1869, 2).

> took his pencil and wrote in bold hand the word "Canada," and I pencilled [sic] my name. We then mounted our waggon [sic], gave three resounding cheers for Her Majesty, and sang, with tears starting to our eyes, "*God Save the Queen.*"[31]

Such a tale recorded the pride at being both Canadian and British and that pride was drawn upon frequently in the pages of the *Canadian Baptist*.

Growing within that national pride was the pressure to colonize the vast expanses of the west before the Americans did. Davidson reported back to Ontario that the United States was well on its way to populating the areas south of the border. He commented: "[Minnesota] is fast filling up, and the American Government is giving land to emigrant settlers on most favourable terms."[32] Implicit in the comment was the threat that if no Canadians filled up the land north of the border, the Americans would most likely turn in that direction for the benefit of their own nation. He wrote, "In what relations will we stand to Great Britain in the matter, if . . . we tamely suffer the territory thus acquired to be betrayed, unintentionally or otherwise, into the hands of a foreign power?"[33] However, if the Canadians could take the land, the Dominion would find new respect and strength in its position. The *Canadian Baptist* printed this excerpt from one of Davidson's lectures: "[If Canadians cultivate the land] we shall soon become a power not antagonistic to, but rival in the

31. Davidson, "Our Journey to Red River," *Canadian Baptist*, 22 July 1869, 2. The popularity of such a sentiment is evidenced in the following remarks, reprinted in response to Davidson's report from the St. John New Brunswick News: "Rather a fine spectacle that of these hat-waving, cheering and anthem singing Baptist divines on the verge of our far western wilderness . . . We should be glad to see ten thousand such men, good to sing, strong to cheer, going into the fertile belt, year by year, for a long time to come" ("Wanted—One Hundred Thousand Baptists in the North-West within the Next Ten Years," *Canadian Baptist*, 14 October 1869, 2).

32. Davidson, "Our Journey to Red River," *Canadian Baptist*, 22 July 1869, 2.

33. Davidson, "The Red River Territory," *Canadian Baptist*, 20 January 1870, 3.

best sense of the word, to our cousins across the line."[34] It was not only competition with America that occupied the columns of the *Canadian Baptist*, but also the need to bring greater civilization to the barbarous plains.[35]

When the Hudson's Bay Company owned the land there was very little effort made to bring outsiders in, since that would have jeopardized the company's hold over the fur trading industry.[36] Davidson commented: "the North West territories are to be governed by Canada and not as heretofore by a fur trading monopoly whose interest it was to discourage immigration into the country and keep it as a howling wilderness."[37] Although there were British and Canadian institutions (including churches)

34. Davidson, "Lecture on the North-West," *Canadian Baptist*, 21 October 1869, 2.

35. "The Protestant missionary was convinced that the Indian, Métis, and Halfbreed were infected by the contagion of barbarism, and that they were lost to civilization" (Pannekoek, *Snug Little Flock*, 80).

36. Articles written in the *Canadian Baptist Register* also mentioned that a similar sentiment existed among the Métis and other Native inhabitants of the land. Whether or not this was an accurate portrayal does not matter, but it was used to further alienate Ontarians from the people of the North West. An example of such sentiments is printed here: "[The inhabitants of the area] do not want the sharp, enterprising competition, which emigration from Ontario must bring; so no loyal feelings are expressed towards our government" (Davidson and Baldwin, "Report of the Deputation of the North West Territories," *Canadian Baptist Register*, 1870, 48). Major Charles Boulton also supported this statement. He wrote: "The Company had one principle, which all the officers rigidly acted upon, namely, to hide from the world any knowledge of the extensive and valuable resources over which they held sway, dreading the influx of an enterprising population, which might wrest from them their valuable fur trade and demoralize the hunting qualities of the Indians" (Boulton, *Reminiscences*, 45). Charlebois, *Life of Louis Riel*, 14–16, also comments on the desire of the Hudson's Bay Company (newly amalgamated with The North-West Company in 1821) to insure their control over the land. He writes: "The fur-traders, united in the Hudson's Bay Company, now confronted a growing and increasingly stronger body of settlers . . . The settlers kept up a continual battle against the Company's attempts to enforce its monopoly."

37. Davidson, "To the North West and Back," *Canadian Baptist*, 19 August 1869, 2.

already established in places like Red River, it was the position of Thomas Davidson that more young Baptist men could bring even greater culture to the uncivilized west. The *Canadian Baptist* printed the following statement:

> [Davidson hoped that the area] would become the future home of our ambitious young men; receive into its broad bosom the surplus millions of the old countries; rearing the spires and domes of civilization; making the Saskatchewan and the Assineboine [sic] echo the music of the Thames and the Mersey; protected by that flag on which the sun never sets.[38]

Statements like that reinforced the idea that bringing Christianity was largely interchangeable with bringing British culture.

Although he was sent by the Baptists as a missionary, Davidson knew the intrinsic value of the land in which he had traveled. He commented numerous times, both in letters and lectures, about the untapped potential of the North West. His reports never ceased making pleas that the Baptist readers look to the west as the place from which they, and the nation of Canada, could draw resources. In one of his lectures Davidson made the following speech:

> [T]he time has already come when those millions upon millions of untilled acres of magnificent prairies can no longer be suffered to lie untilled, when those far-stretching rivers and quiet lakes must be navigated not alone by the frail Indian canoe, but they must be ploughed by our noble steamers bearing the produce of well tilled lands, of the almost boundless mineral resources of the far West and proudly floating the Old Flag. The pathway to empire lies Westward and is open to our New Dominion.[39]

Although such sentiments were no doubt compelling, Davidson and Baldwin used most of their space reporting what they saw, not what they thought.

38. Davidson, "Lecture on the North-West," *Canadian Baptist*, 7 October 1869, 3.

39. Davidson, "Lecture on the North-West," *Canadian Baptist*, 21 October 1869, 2.

The land itself was the major selling point, and this is evidenced by the large number of articles simply extolling its value and fertility, and the amount of space the land received in the pages of the *Register*. The *Canadian Baptist* printed this comment: "All things considered, this country, from Fort Garry southward along the Red River for 60 miles to the boundary line . . . is a most desirable place for settlement."[40] Upon their return from the west, Davidson and Baldwin toured Ontario pleading their case and drawing large crowds of curious people. Although we no longer possess the content of their lectures, the responses printed in the *Canadian Baptist* and the *Register* seem to indicate that the presentations were entertaining, enlightening, and well-attended.[41] They also seem to have been designed to educate people, in the hopes that they would decide to settle out west. Shortly after their return, the *Canadian Baptist* printed this report about one of Davidson's lectures: "The Baptist Chapel and Vestry, seats and standing room, were densely crowded . . . [this was due to] the interest now felt on the subject by most thoughtful and patriotic persons."[42] It is worth noting that the paper mentions that the event was "densely crowded," that the subject was gathering interest, and commends those who attended as both "thoughtful" and "patriotic."

Davidson appears to have done the lion's share of the lectures; he also appears to have been very engaging. The

40. Davidson, "Great North West Territories," *Canadian Baptist*, 14 October 1869, 2.

41. It is on this point that I part company with others who have written on the subject at hand. Although never explicitly stated, it has been largely the consensus of other historians that the Baptist mission to the west never had much momentum behind it. However, after the return of Davidson and Baldwin, it appears, based on articles in the *Canadian Baptist*, that their lectures and writing were immensely popular. While it cannot be stated definitively whether or not Baptists would have moved west earlier had the Riel incident not occurred, it is worth noting that prior to the event the idea of western expansion was gaining in popularity.

42. Davidson, "Lecture on the North-West" *Canadian Baptist*, 7 October 1869, 3.

Canadian Baptist reported that he frequently made use of props to further enamor his audience with the western lands:

> On the platform beside the speaker, during the lecture, was a large trunk, and from time to time, by way of illustration, came specimens of wheat, prairie grass, rank and luxuriant, prairie flowers, Indian curiosities (not scalps, the Reds prized them too highly to part with them) . . . and a few pounds of pemmican, or Buffalo meat, prepared without salt to keep in any climate.[43]

Such demonstrations were designed to capture the imagination of the people as well as eliminate certain fears. The efforts of these two men were being rewarded and the notion that Baptists could move out west was gaining momentum. Not only was the venture becoming popular but the conclusions reached by Davidson and Baldwin included the need for expediency in seeing the move west realized. They finished their official report by writing the following:

> In conclusion, permit us to express it as our opinion, in view of all the circumstances, that the conditional appointment of a missionary, providing a colony of Baptist families would unite, move and settle together, in the Great North-West; would be a means of spreading Baptist principles in that far off country, *faster than by any other way within our reach*.[44]

However, all that was to change shortly after the men's return, for while they were still touring and defending their case, the land they were extolling exploded into chaos and violence.[45]

43. Davidson, "Lecture on the North-West," *Canadian Baptist*, 7 October 1869, 3.

44. Davidson and Baldwin, "Report of the Deputation of the North West Territories," *Canadian Baptist Register*, 1870, 51–52 (italics added for emphasis).

45. While we know little of Baldwin's activities outside of lecturing at this time, we do know that Davidson's absence from his church during the latter half of 1869 was used by some to remove him from his office. Upon his return Davidson had been convinced that his church would do better without him and that he should resign. The official feelings of the church reflected this to be not true but the following quote from the Aylmer Baptist Church Minutes, 12 December, 1869, serves the purpose of the topic at hand by showing that

Davidson and Baldwin returned to Ontario in late 1869; had they stayed they would have had far more to write home about. Political insurrection was afoot in Red River and the events that transpired after their return to Ontario completely overshadowed all the positive press they had attempted to bring to the North West. The rebellion was crucial, because once Fort Garry was taken and the Canadian surveyors were prevented from entering the territory,[46] all mention about Baptists moving west halted,[47] as did the flow of reliable information. From that point on the *Canadian Baptist*'s stance on the North West was reduced to editorializing about the incident, arguments about misappropriation of the funds used to pay Davidson and Baldwin,[48] and

Davidson was in personal conflict during his time on the road: ". . . we as a church do not believe the work and usefulness of Rev. Dr. Davidson is done in this Church and community as stated in his resignation . . . the statement made by parties at a distance and not connected with this Church to the affect that this Church would be glad for the Rev. Dr. Davidson to leave us is utterly false."

46. "By the time the Governor [MacDougall] arrived in Pembina [Riel] had a small force under his command, at River Sale, where he erected a barricade to guard the entrance into the country . . . Riel, finding that the Governor had ignored his warning . . . sent a party to drive him across the line by force, if necessary" (Boulton, *Reminiscences,* 63).

47. Historian Hartwell Bowsfield also refers to the idea of destiny present in the Ontario mindset as it pertained to emigration to what would become Manitoba. He also cites the Riel uprising as the incident that threatened the move more than anything else. Bowsfield writes: "It was expected that the new western provinces which would eventually emerge should resemble the one from which settlers were most likely to come. But the Riel disturbance in 1869–1870 threatened to defeat Ontario's declared destiny" (Bowsfield, *Riel*, 62).

48. Throughout 1870 there were several articles printed under the title "Red River Deputation," that chronicled the debate between A. T. Wood and certain members of the Baptist Convention that he charged with misappropriation of funds. The money for the missionaries to the area was still short about $75 by January of 1870. Money was supposed to be raised to pay them by those who had supported the enterprise to the North West, but the goal had not been met. The argument was that other missionaries needed to know that they could trust the Convention to supply them with the financial means they needed. He also argued that people would stop paying into this fund if the money was

printing second-hand reports about the insurgence that often proved to be false.

The situation in Red River officially began in December of 1869 when Louis Riel and some Métis followers took possession of Fort Garry after the Hudson's Bay Company relinquished control of the Red River Settlement to the Canadian government.[49] Concerned that the existing land allotments would not be honored, the Métis were resistant to the deal because the land they lived on had been sold without their consent. The Baptist explorer, Davidson, wrote the following in the *Canadian Baptist* to help the readers understand the Métis's perspective. He wrote: "[The Métis] are considerably discontented just now, and the cause of this is that they say the Hudson's Bay Company have sold them and their country to the Canadian Government."[50]

Little had been done by Canada to assuage the Métis's fear and Davidson proved fairly prophetic when he proclaimed that trouble would come if the government did not make dealing with the native inhabitants its first concern. He wrote:

> In my humble opinion the *first imperative* duty of the Government is to make a treaty . . . with the present owners of the soil . . . The Government are now making a serious mistake, and I tremble for the probable results. Surveyors are now sent out to survey the land before it is bought from the Indians, thus rousing their ire.[51]

The Métis, though demonized as violent and resistant to Canada, frequently stated that their only concern regarding the Canadian agenda in the northwest was that the officials sent to represent the new nation did not seem to acknowledge the

misappropriated. This debate carried on well into the spring of 1870. Also, in this article Davidson and Baldwin are referred to as missionaries.

49. "The terms of this agreement were a money payment of three hundred thousand pounds, and one-twentieth of the lands as they were surveyed, to be selected by the Company within fifty years, also a reservation around each of their principal posts throughout the country" (Boulton, *Reminiscenses*, 51).

50. Davidson, "The Great North-West," *Canadian Baptist*, 2 September 1869, 2.

51. Davidson, "The Great North West: Its Present Drawbacks and Disadvantages," *Canadian Baptist*, 16 September 1869, 2.

existing allotments. The *Canadian Baptist* recorded similar sentiments when reports became available from the settlement. One article recorded the following: "The Red River rebellion has at length pegged out. It was a humbug all the way through. These half-breeds never sought Independence, much less Annexation. They were dissatisfied from fear that they might lose the title lands on which they squatted."[52]

In one of his letters, Louis Riel wrote about the lack of regard the inhabitants were shown by the Canadians. He wrote: "under the orders of General Dennis, government surveyors arrived and began drawing lines in every direction, totally disregarding the fact that they were on private property."[53] Even earlier on in 1868 Riel made the following comment that shows the level of distrust the Métis had for the Canadian government. He stated: "As soon as winter [of 1868] set in, the Canadian Government, under the pretext of supplying relief to the Red River families threatened by famine, had sent some workers to open the Dawson Road at Points-de-Chenes. That was the first infraction. The country was not Canadian, and this was an unprecedented act for a government to do."[54]

Sprague, in his article "The Manitoba Land Question, 1870–1882," commented on what he perceived to be the duplicity of the Manitoba Land Act. He believed that the Act was simply a ploy to keep the peace while the Canadian government recreated the entire area in Ontario's likeness. He writes: "The leading members of the government believed that Canada could—and should—change the face of the province they recognized in 1870, to recreate Manitoba in the image of Ontario."[55] The idea

52. "The North-West," *Canadian Baptist*, 17 February 1870, 2. It is also worth noticing that the author of this quote mentions that the original inhabitants were "squatting" on the land and this person was also wrong when he/she stated that the entire ordeal was over in February; when the Canadian military marched into Red River in August, that is when the Provisional government was replaced by the Canadian government.

53. Fremont, quoting Riel, in *Secretaries of Riel*, 14.

54. Ibid.

55. Sprague, "Manitoba Land Question," 63.

of using laws familiar to the people of Ontario to remove the native inhabitants of Red River was something that the *Canadian Baptist* reported to its readers as well in the months before the rebellion. The native distaste for the Canadian system of taxation would be used to drive them from the lands Ontarians wanted to possess. One such article stated: "The half-breeds will not submit to taxation, and the result will be that they will sell out their claims to Canadians and move back on unsurveyed lands, and hence, in a few years, settlers from Canada and elsewhere will own the lands they now control."[56] Sentiments such as this further showed a desire to colonize the west for the purposes of the citizens of Ontario but the desire to bring their culture to the west was hampered by Riel's plans, and his violent refusal to accept Canadian dominance made him a serious obstacle to the Baptist mission.

In response to the taking of Fort Garry, the Canadians tried to gain support for their cause from other Red River inhabitants. The *Canadian Baptist* tried to show its readers that Riel's group held very little sway over the greater population of Red River. It reported: "The Provisional Government is said to be very unpopular even among its former supporters. It only commands the support of a section of the half-breed population, and they are impatient of anything like discipline or military restraint."[57] The Anglophone settlers in the region seemed a natural selection for the Canadians to recruit, but the English and French had peacefully coexisted for years in Red River and this cohabitation proved to be an insurmountable obstacle to Colonel Dennis's plan.[58] His inability to raise a formidable army gave strength to Riel's Provisional Government. Louis Schmidt wrote in his journal: "Colonel Dennis, for his part, was probing to find out if it would be possible to levy an army among the English and

56. Davidson, "The Great North-West," *Canadian Baptist*, 2 September 1869, 2.

57. "Red River," *Canadian Baptist*, 10 June 1870, 3.

58. Dennis was MacDougall's right hand man and was given charge over the area by MacDougall to remove Riel from Red River.

Scottish settlers to fight the French Métis. The results were disconcerting."[59]

With the Métis firmly in control of Red River and the military unable to forcefully dislodge them, getting accurate details about the insurrection back to Ontario became nearly impossible. The *Canadian Baptist* struggled to find reliable information for its readers and came up woefully short in this regard. The distance between Ontario and Red River became apparent as all information about the battle came to the *Canadian Baptist* via other sources. Articles that spoke of Riel's failures one month were retracted the next. One such example took place in early 1870; in the issue of 3 February it was reported that Riel was arrested and his staunch supporters had all but deserted him. This was no doubt received as good news in Ontario. However, the following week the *Canadian Baptist* was forced to report that mail and newspapers had just come in from Red River, "neither of which mention the arrest of Riel."[60] In addition to that, the *Canadian Baptist* reported that Riel's popularity had not vanished but was actually growing. The *Canadian Baptist* wrote: "The opposition party of the French has all gone over to Riel, and now want to invest him with supreme power . . . Riel proposes then to employ all his powers and resources to carry out the programme of his adherents; which is anti-Canadian to the last."[61] Even the last statement about Riel's anti-Canadian agenda proved to be false as well. He simply wanted to insure that the rights of the people

59. Fremont, *Secretaries of Riel*, 16. Charlebois also notes how ethnic disparity between the Scottish settlers and the Métis was prominent and traced its roots back to the early days of the Red River Settlement. He writes: "The North-West employees did their best to incite the Métis and Indians against the new Scottish settlers, making use of differences of race, religion and national origin, to create an animosity which was to last for many years" (*Life of Louis Riel*, 13). What is most amazing about this incident is that, by the time of Riel's rebellion, the different groups had actually learned to live so peacefully with each other, even to the point that they refused to fight one another!

60. "Red River Settlement," *Canadian Baptist*, 10 February 1870, 2.

61. "Red River Settlement," *Canadian Baptist*, 10 February 1870, 2.

of Red River would be respected under the governance of Canada.

However, it must be considered that something more sinister than simply inaccurate fact-gathering was going on here. The press was instrumental in maintaining Riel's status as a crook and enemy of Canada and vilifying him became essential to maintaining support in Ontario. The loyalism of Ontario was highlighted as the Métis were held up as traitors to Canada.[62] Sprague records the delineation between loyalists and insurgents in the wake of the situation during a census of the area. He writes: "while enumerating Manitobans for census purposes in the autumn of 1870, the population was sorted into two groups, one the 'Insurgents' and the other the 'Loyalists.' Loyalists received cash indemnities and political patronage. There was nothing for the general Insurgent population."[63] Historian J. M. Bumsted also charges the press of the time with deliberately reporting false stories designed to incite Protestant anger in Ontario. He states: "the main effect of the propaganda campaign was to inflame Protestant Ontario against Louis Riel and the Métis."[64] The *Canadian Illustrated News* seemed to support this accusation when they wrote the following editorial: "acrimonious and insulting attacks upon the people of Red River should not be indulged by the press."[65]

Throughout the pages of the *Canadian Baptist*, Riel was constantly portrayed as a criminal and a man of ill repute. While loyalism was not as prominent a theme, the *Baptist* revealed its Christian roots by accusing Riel and his followers of questionable morality. Several blatantly inflammatory articles were printed that were designed to call into question the character of the leaders of the Métis uprising. One of Riel's officers was a man by the name of O'Donohue and the *Canadian Baptist* reported

62. This was even though they were not actually citizens of Canada and, as such, could not be considered traitors to a country to which they had yet to belong.

63. Sprague, "Manitoba Land Question," 64.

64. Bumsted (ed.), *Reporting the Resistance*, 171.

65. Sean Sullivan, *Canadian Illustrated News*, 25 June 1870, 534.

that he was even more sinister than his famous leader: "O'Donohue is still more generally execrated than Riel, as he is deemed, if possible, more shameless. His last exploit was to steal money from a letter addressed to Mrs. Mair, who is still in the settlement. He also wears Mrs. Schultz's gold watch."[66]

Ironically, the one incident which most supported the *Canadian Baptist*'s claims of Riel's moral repugnancy warranted little attention. The execution of Orangeman[67] Thomas Scott under Riel's leadership was viewed by many as Riel's fatal political blunder that ultimately led to his exile from Canada and the collapse of his Provisional Government.[68] Fremont makes the following quote: "starting from that day . . . Riel's power, even among his own people, started to diminish until at last he remained almost alone."[69] However, the only time the *Canadian Baptist* mentioned this watershed moment was to question whether or not the event had even occurred. The *Baptist* wrote the following: "Not more than half the settlers profess to believe that

66. "Red River," *Canadian Baptist*, 26 May 1870, 3. O'Donoghue (note the different spelling) would actually help command a Fenian force into Manitoba after a falling out with Riel because he thought Riel was too compromising to the British. Riel never supported the Fenian invasion and saw them as unconcerned with the affairs of the Métis. The two parted company and it is possible that Riel actually led a cavalry charge against O'Donoghue in 1871 when the Fenians actually did invade. There will be more on the Fenian invasion in a subsequent section of this paper.

67. The Orangemen and Orange Lodge were named after William of Orange, the Protestant king who replaced James II in 1691 and insured that the British throne would remain Protestant. The Orangemen were virulent opponents of anything Catholic (which most Métis were) and staunch loyalists.

68. Evidence of just how serious a blunder this execution was considered is the following quote from Riel's personal secretary, Louis Schmidt, during this time: "I will not try to justify that execution. For years it was used by the people of Ontario to foster their prejudice and hatred, not only against the Métis but against everything French and Catholic . . . Scott's execution, under the circumstances, remained none the less a very grave political error . . . It was the signal for an unfortunate upheaval that was to degenerate into a conflict of race and religion with long and painful repercussions" (Fremont, *Secretaries of Riel*, 39–40.

69. Fremont, quoting Alexander Begg, *Secretaries of Riel*, 40.

Scott was killed, and it is deemed treason to mention the subject."[70] Of all the false reports issued in the *Canadian Baptist*, the only one they questioned was the one that turned out to be true. It would not be until the end of the situation, when evidence was more readily available, that Scott would be elevated to the status of martyr for the Canadian cause.[71] Riel was held up as a tyrant with Scott playing the part of noble loyalist. One article, written in England and reprinted in the *Canadian Baptist*, commented: "an adventurer has risen to power, called himself President, plundered private property, and murdered one, who, loyal to the last, denied a spurious rule."[72]

A large portion of the press of the time seemed concerned only with creating an image of Riel that was designed to breed rage and distrust within the minds of Ontario readers. This, obviously, had an impact on the minds of Baptists in Ontario and their proposed mission west. Rather than reporting the Canadian government's attempts to incite civil war within the Red River settlement in order to take the land from the natives by force, the press deliberately set Riel up as an enemy of the new nation of Canada. The instability Riel's insurrection brought to the region played to Ontarians' desire to see Canada grow stronger and more prosperous. In an article in May of 1870 the *Canadian*

70. "Red River," *Canadian Baptist*, 26 May 1870, 2.

71. The relationship between Scott and Riel took on almost mythical qualities in certain arenas of Canadian life. In the anonymous book *The Story of Louis Riel: The Rebel Chief* (1885), is an account that Scott and Riel met much earlier than the insurrection. In the tale, Riel became enamoured of a young farm girl he met while hunting in the woods. When she did not return his affections, Riel assumed that she had another love interest. Riel stayed with the girl and her father and the next morning he caught her looking out the window at a "tall, well-formed, young white man." Figuring this to be the man who had the young maiden's heart, Riel found out that it was none other than Thomas Scott. The author of the book then records: "This was the same Scott . . . the tidings of whose fate, at the hands of the rebel and murderer, Louis Riel, in later years, sent the blood boiling through the veins of Western Canada." Thus the seeds of enmity were planted between the two men long before their fateful (and more historical) encounter during the Red River Rebellion. For more, see *The Story of Louis Riel*, 49–62.

72. "Red River Difficulty," *Canadian Baptist*, 3 September 1870, 2.

Baptist reminded people that Riel's antics practically invited foreign invaders like the Irish-American Fenians into the open expanse of the west.[73]

According to Sprague, national pride also played a vital role in the mentality of Protestant Ontario towards Riel. He writes: "Ontario members of Parliament—especially those with Orange Lodge Associations—complained that Canada had been humiliated. National honour demanded punishment rather than favours for these western rebels."[74] However, the *Canadian Baptist* was not so forthright in its assessment of Red River, and an author known simply as "Querist" lobbied the newspaper, hoping that cooler and less violent heads would prevail. He wrote:

> [That] the resources of honorable and statesmanlike diplomacy should be brought to bear and exhausted, before any sterner alternative is proposed, must be admitted by any patriotic and christian [sic] mind . . . It cannot surely be contended that [The Hudson's Bay Company] were in any way bound to transfer the *allegiance* of the half-breeds, or that the *inhabitants* were in any sense included in the terms of the sale. But if we bought simply certain Territorial rights, or claims with encumbrances, can we honorably recede from our engagements because those encumbrances prove a little more troublesome, possibly through our own fault, than we supposed?[75]

Although this quote is conciliatory in nature it is worth noting that in the same article Querist also reminded the readers that the government was established by God to maintain order on earth, and, if need be, must use the sword. Querist's article ended with the following words:

73. "Our sons would have to leave their farms, workshops and stores, not only for Indian warfare in western wilds, but also to face Fenians and other reckless adventurers in our own country" ("Script of the Canadian Literary Institute," *Canadian Baptist*, 27 January 1870, 3). This prophecy regarding the Fenians entrance into this land would prove accurate. See below.

74. Sprague, "Manitoba Land Question," 63.

75. Querist, "The Red River Territory," *Canadian Baptist*, 20 January 1870, 3.

> If human governments are of Divine appointment, is is [sic] it not their first duty to be a "terror to evil-doers and a praise to them that do well." And ought not the religious sentiment, and religious press of the country to encourage, and impel them, to the adoption of such gentle, just, yet firm and unequivocal measures, as are after all the only safeguards of liberty, peace and prosperity? A vacillating and timid policy never yet made a peaceable and prosperous nation.[76]

This statement began a debate within the pages of the *Canadian Baptist* which lasted two more months.

Those who opposed Querist restated that involvement in a violent confrontation could open the expansive and not well-armed Dominion to other hostile forces. However, while that was a legitimate concern, the *Canadian Baptist* was a Christian magazine and the final word was a commendation to put the matter into the hands of God, and to remember that the God the Baptists served was never in favor of war:

> Let not the Patriotism of "Querist" blind his mind to the fact that the Dominion of Canada, aside from the Mother Country, is a small nation. Boast as we may of our resources, they are to be enjoyed in peace . . . [if it comes to war] turbulent spirits, the offspring of old world revolutions, and of the late American war, would swarm upon our borders. Our sons would have to leave their farms, workshops and stores, not only for Indian warfare in western wilds, but also to face Fenians and other reckless adventurers in our own country. We advise 'Querist' to cool down, and let statesmanship, under the guidance of an All Wise Over-Ruling Providence, solve the problem of the future relationship which we shall sustain to the North-West. "My voice is not for war."[77]

It is worth noting, in light of Bumsted's condemnation of the press's lack of objectivity, that Querist commends the press to exert influence on its readers and its government to insure that the situation finds a proper, Christian conclusion.

76. Querist, "The Red River Territory," *Canadian Baptist*, 20 January 1870, 3.

77. "Script of the Canadian Literary Institute," *Canadian Baptist*, 27 January 1870, 3.

It would be unfair to say that the *Canadian Baptist* spent all of its power to demonize Riel; the truth is that after the end of the Red River situation and Riel's exile to the United States,[78] the *Baptist* also reported discontent with regards to the manner in which the press had acted during the disturbance. The following statement appeared:

> A long editorial headed "Right or Wrong" goes on to prove that the Red River people have always been loyal, and have been misunderstood—that the English and Canadian press begin to acknowledge this, and that the surrendering of the Government by the Hudson Bay Company on the arrival of Mr. McDougall made it necessary that a Provisional Government should be formed.[79]

The Protestant press exerted a tremendous amount of influence over its people at this time and the opinions expressed within the pages of the *Canadian Baptist* had an unmatched ability to influence the opinions of its readers.[80] Comments like that would have been absolutely vital to begin the process of rebuilding peace and goodwill between the Canadians and the Métis as well as getting the Baptist mission to the west back on track.

The *Canadian Baptist*'s push to see more Baptists out west completely relaxed during the Red River situation. In 1869, every article relating to the west recorded the concern that there was no Baptist presence west of Ontario and sought to remedy that problem. It was apparent that many people still held on to

78. "Red River Matters," *Canadian Baptist*, 18 August 1870, mentions Riel briefly and wonders whether or not he is worth sending people after him. Some argue that the US and Canada should both find him.

79. "Red River Matters," *Canadian Baptist*, 30 June 1870, 2.

80. Peter Henessy notes that papers were given over to editorializing and how accurately they portrayed the mindset of their readers must be scrutinized. For more on this see Hennessy, "The Press and Broadcasting," 20. Even though journalists cannot be expected to treat issues of the day with as even a hand as historians, the usefulness to historians of newspapers to help define the positions of certain people within a given community cannot be underestimated. For more on this topic see Heath, "Forming Sound Public Opinion," footnotes 10 and 11; Franzosi, "The Press as a Source," 5–16.

fears of the uncivilized expanse beyond Ontario's borders and the Riel incident did nothing to quell those fears. Baldwin and Davidson tried to remedy that when they wrote: "In the absence of any regular form of government, or the administration of law, it is marvellous [sic] that such good order is maintained in and beyond the Red River Settlement, that crime is so little known, and quiet is so generally maintained."[81] They also tried to instill in their readers confidence in the institutions present in the west by writing, "The Hudson Bay Company claim to govern within 50 miles of Fort Garry; they have a council, judge, and gaol."[82] However, the Red River situation rendered all such assertions of safety and peace moot.

To make matters worse, while the Riel situation was still present, a new fear materialized on the North Western expanse: Fenians. Although the Fenian raid on Manitoba would not happen until the next year, in the spring of 1870 articles were appearing in the *Baptist* that all but promised imminent violence from the despised Irish-Americans. Davidson and Baldwin had used the wide-open expanse of the west as a motivating factor to bring Baptists in but now the lack of ability to defend Red River could be seen as a deterrent. The *Baptist* wrote: "[Fenians are] mustering . . . in various parts of Minnesota, and one party is now en route overland. There is now at St. Paul a Fenian force of about 300, awaiting arrangements for transportation and subsistence before commencing the march to Red River."[83] Adding to the apprehension about heading west were reports that as the military went to Red River, the Fenians would simply switch their target from the North West to Toronto and Montreal. The

81. Davidson and Baldwin, "The Great North West," *Canadian Baptist*, 12 August 1869, 2.

82. Davidson and Baldwin, "Report of the Deputation of the North West Territories," *Canadian Baptist Register*, 1870, 48.

83. "Fenians and Red River," *The Canadian Baptist*, 19 May 1870, 3. The Baptists also used this as an opportunity to condemn what they thought was cowardly and negligent behavior on the part of the American government. The following quote is an example: "This opportunity [the raid] would not have been afforded if the United States authorities had done their duty in season" ("The Fenian Raid," *The Canadian Baptist*, 2 June 1870, 3).

fears of a Fenian takeover of Canada are present in the following quote:

> A portion of the regular force had been recalled to England, and a large detachment of those left had already begun the march Red Riverward. This was the moment of all others for a Fenian invasion, and had these deluded Irishmen been led by men of the average ability of school boys, they would, as we have said, penetrated to the very verge of the metropolis of the Dominion.[84]

Although this comment is blatantly condescending to the Fenians, it appears that there existed awareness that if the Fenians ever got capable leadership they could do some real damage. The idea that Ontario could be taken while its citizens moved west could do nothing to advance the Baptist mission.[85]

84. "Red River Difficulty," *The Canadian Baptist*, 23 June 1870, 3. When the Fenian threat actually materialized in October of 1871 it did more to undermine the Fenians than cause fear in the hearts of the Canadians. The Fenians took a fort at Pembina but ran out of supplies and went back across the border without incident. Volunteers from all over the region came together to challenge the Fenians but the two armies never met. There was no battle, no bloodshed, and the Fenian threat was extinguished, never to appear again. Had it not been for the victory at Limeridge and the taking of Ft. Erie in 1866, the Fenians would have been nothing more than a bad joke to the Canadians. But, since the 1866 incident, the Canadians did take any Fenian threats seriously. For more on the Churches and the Fenian threat of 1866, see Robertson, "A Very Present Help."

85. There is one threat that also materialized and would have been detrimental to the Baptist mission but since it received very little coverage in the press I have chosen to restrict it to the footnotes. Since the land was seen as incredibly valuable, Baldwin and Davidson were concerned about potential threats to its productivity. During the course of their travels one threat seemed to stand above the rest: grasshoppers. Davidson made this comment: "everything depends, so to speak, on the grasshoppers. If they visit the settlements this year and do the work of utter devastation they did last year, immigration from Canada will be checked and many who are now in the country will leave it" (Davidson, "The Great North-West," *Canadian Baptist*, 2 September 1869, 2). After the insurrection it appears that the fears of Davidson and Baldwin came true. Although there is no mention as to what kind of damage was done, there were reports that grasshoppers were in abundance on the prairie around Red River. The *Canadian Baptist* reported: "There is but little news for the North-

Another way the Riel insurgence impacted the Baptist mission was that animosity towards Catholics, which was noticeably absent in 1869, reared up in 1870. The Baptists had always lamented the fact that other denominations had traveled west before they had, but during the insurrection the Catholic Church was singled out as a potential obstruction to the improvement of the west. The Métis's French ethnicity was also bitterly referenced. One issue recorded the following sentiment:

> [Manitoba is in] the hands of *French*—not even *Canadian*—priests, which will place the most stubborn if not the most insurmountable barrier in the way of opening up and improving that Western country . . . It is not easy to conceive a more non-improveable [sic] or non progressive people than Roman Catholic priests and half-breeds.[86]

Since the Catholics were the dominant religious influence among the Métis[87] the Roman Church became an easy target for the Baptist press. The *Register* lamented Baptist tardiness in getting to the frontier and openly acknowledged that the wasted time would create more work in establishing a Baptist presence. At the end of the year it was recorded, "The labour of the denomination has been increased perhaps ten fold by its tardiness of action in regard to mission work in the beginning of villages, towns, and cities."[88]

The Baptist mission to the west was usurped by the political reality of the land it had been attempting to convince its readers was peaceful and safe. There was little point in "selling" the west to its readership while someone like Riel was in control. During

West and traders report business quiet and everything status quo. The *New Nation* of the 8th says: Grasshoppers have appeared in many parts of the settlement; they almost cover the face of the earth . . . it is impossible to foretell the extent of the damage they may yet cause" ("The Scourge of Grasshoppers: Manitoba," *Canadian Baptist*, 28 July 1870, 2).

86. "The Political Situation," *Canadian Baptist*, 26 May 1870, 3.

87. "Of the 14,000 inhabitants, not less than 5,000 or 6,000 are Roman Catholics; priestcraft dates coeval with the Settlement itself" (Davidson and Baldwin, "Report of the Deputation of the North West Territories," *Canadian Baptist Register*, 1870, 49).

88. Davidson and Baldwin, "Report of the Deputation of the North West Territories," *Canadian Baptist Register*, 1870, 51.

those few months the *Canadian Baptist* decided to put the topic on the back burner and used its influence to inform its readers about the most recent struggle embroiling the nation of Canada. The facts gathered by the *Baptist* were spurious at best and while the paper was not hesitant to impugn Riel's character it did reflect an internal struggle within the Baptist Church on which course of action best suited the conflict. Most editorials were designed to paint Riel as an unpopular criminal perpetually on the brink of defeat and none were supportive of Riel or his government.

At the conclusion of the insurgence in the summer of 1870, the *Canadian Baptist* and *Register* showed little interest in returning to the topic of western emigration. The 1871 *Register* did not even mention the North West once and the *Baptist* switched its focus from Riel to Napoleon for the course of the year. Although there are occasional mentions of the western territory, they are few and far between and lack the drive of their pre-rebellion counterparts.

However, just over a year after the Riel situation ended, mention of Baptists in the west began to re-emerge. W. J. Copp of Hamilton apparently took the cause of the western expansion up and proposed that the issue be raised again. The *Baptist* printed the following statement:

> [T]he following resolution was passed, after having been highly recommended by several able speeches: "That we give our candid and serious attention to the propriety of forwarding Bro. Copp's movement to send a Missionary to Manitoba, inasmuch as we do not wish our beloved denomination, and the principles to which we so tenaciously cling, to go unrepresented in that region."[89]

While the cause was working its way back to the front, the focus had changed from promoting the safety and beauty of the land to encouraging a sense of adventure and a willingness to endure dangers for the sake of the Gospel. The following quote

89. "Communications: Manitoba," *Canadian Baptist*, 28 September 1871, 2.

is an example: "We require a man, or *men*, who are fearless in *attack* and *able* to, 'push the battle to the gates'; then success is covenanted and sure."[90] In order to combat those who might bring financial concerns to bear on the matter it was proposed to find 100 Baptist families who would contribute ten dollars for three years to cover the cost of sending a missionary to the west.

The *Register*, after a year hiatus from the topic, also began to approach the subject. In the 1872 issue the following appeared:

> In this, as the best connection, we record the fact that a Committee, consisting of Revs. Dr. Fyfe, John Torrance and others, was appointed to consider the duty of the Baptists of Ontario, to send a Missionary or Missionaries to Manitoba, at as early a day as possible. The Committee had a lengthened and earnest conference on the subject.[91]

Although this quote may seem to be about little more than discussion, it is worth noting that in the next year's *Register* the choice of a missionary for the North West was finally made. The following was recorded, "Rev. Dr Fyfe, chairman of the Committee appointed to select a missionary for Manitoba, reported that the services of Rev. Alexander MacDonald, of Sparta, had been secured."[92] The steps were small and late in coming but the signs were clear: the mission to the west had returned.

In conclusion, the power of the Baptist press was put to use to insure the spread of the Baptist message to the largely unexplored North West Territory throughout 1869 and 1870. Using biblical imagery, appeals to evangelism and national prosperity, fear of American domination, imperialism, and the fertility of the land, the Baptist Church attempted to influence its members to look west in hopes of further increasing the Baptist influence on the Canadian landscape. However, the Riel insurrection, more than any other factor, derailed the Baptist attempt at western emigration because it undermined the positive traits that

90. Ibid. (italics part of the original quote).

91. "Committee on Missions to Manitoba," *Canadian Baptist Register*, October 1872, 17.

92. "Mission to Manitoba," *Canadian Baptist Register*, October, 1873, 15–16.

Davidson and Baldwin had attempted to bring to the potentially dangerous and fearsome expedition. The evidence of the unstable political climate in the land overshadowed the conjecture and words of the two missionaries in much the same way as Joshua and Caleb's words fell on deaf Israelite ears after the people heard the reports of giants in their own Promised Land. The reports of Riel's rebellion and the Métis's violent ways brought what was originally a popular idea to a halt. Those who wanted to see the western expansion materialize were forced to change their focus in the wake of the troubles of 1869–1870. C. C. McLaurin, writing on this topic, made the following comments:

> Political turmoil was another condition which did nothing to help the work of our early missionaries in Western Canada. Peaceful, happy, domestic life was well nigh impossible . . . During all this turmoil [Riel] the Baptists in Ontario were making plans. Missionaries of other religious bodies were arriving, settlers were pouring into the country, and churches were being established. This uncertain state of "law and order" retarded the settlement of the country for a time.[93]

Thus the focus of the *Baptist* from 1871 was less on personal or national gain and more on brave people going to spread the Gospel of Christ in a foreign land.

Whereas problems with finances and within the Ontario Home Mission cannot be forgotten, the gap from 1869—when the mission was first brought to the fore—until the first residential missionary set foot on western ground in 1873, is best explained by the instability of the region in question. After all, once the area had calmed for a time and the motion was back on the table the western expansion moved along with no further stops.

Alexander "Pioneer" MacDonald did tremendous work in Red River and beyond. Baptists responded to the idea of supporting the mission for three years out of their own pockets quite

93. McLaurin, *Pioneering in Western Canada*, 61–63.

positively; other ministers began to arrive[94] and in 1879 a former Roman Catholic priest by the name of A. C. Turner was the first Baptist minister ordained in the west. In 1880 the Red River Baptist Association was formed, which included a church from Riel's former stronghold in Fort Garry.[95] Although the Baptist growth in the west was not rapid, their presence was entrenched and the land that had once been nothing more than a howling wilderness was on its way to becoming the garden the Baptist Church had hoped it might become.

Bibliography

Berger, Carl. *The Sense of Power: Studies in the Ideas of Canadian Imperialism, 1867–1914*. Toronto: University of Toronto Press, 1970.

Boulton, Charles A. *Reminiscences of the North-West Rebellions with a Record of the Raising of Her Majesty's 100th Regiment in Canada*. Toronto: Grip Printing and Publishing Company, 1886.

Bowsfield, Hartwell (ed.). *Louis Riel: Selected Readings*. Toronto: Copp Clark Pitman, 1988.

Bumsted, J. M. *The Red River Rebellion*. Winnipeg: Manitoba Arts Council, 1996.

———. (ed.) *Reporting the Resistance: Alexander Begg and Joseph Hargrave on the Red River Resistance*. Winnipeg: University of Manitoba Press, 2003.

94. Most notably William Murden, who worked north of Winnipeg in and around the town of Gladstone.

95. For more on the development of the Red River Association see Renfree, *Heritage and Horizon*, 176. By then Fort Garry was known as Winnipeg and the other three churches were Emerson, Stonewall, and High Bluff.

Campey, Lucille H. *The Silver Chief: Lord Selkirk and the Scottish Pioneers of Belfast, Baldoon and Red River*. Toronto: Natural Heritage Books, 2003.

Charlebois, Peter. *The Life of Louis Riel*. Toronto: NC Press, 1975.

Coutts, Robert. *The Road to the Rapids: Nineteenth Century Church and Society at St. Andrew's Parish, Red River*. Calgary: University of Calgary Press, 2000.

Franzosi, Roberto. "The Press as a Source of Socio-Historical Data: Issues in the Methodology of Data Collection from Newspapers." *Historical Methods* (1987) 5–16.

Fremont, Donatien. *The Secretaries of Riel*. Prince-Albert: La Société Canadienne Francaise, 1985.

Grant, John Webster. *The Church in the Canadian Era*. Vancouver: Regent College Publishing, 1988.

Heath, Gordon. "'Forming Sound Public Opinion': The Late Victorian Canadian Protestant Press and Nation-Building." *Journal of the Canadian Church Historical Society* (forthcoming), footnotes 10 and 11.

Hennessy, Peter. "The Press and Broadcasting." In *Contemporary History: Practice and Method*, edited by Anthony Seldon, 17–29. Oxford: Blackwell, 1988.

Huel, Raymond (ed.). *The Collected Writings of Louis Riel*. Vol. 1, *1867–1875*. Edmonton: University of Alberta Press, 1985.

McLaurin, C. C. *Pioneering in Western Canada: A Story of the Baptists*. Calgary: published by the author, 1939.

Messamore, Barbara J. *Canada's Governor General: Biography and Constitutional Evolution, 1847–1878.* Toronto: University of Toronto Press, 2006.

Pannekoek, Frits. *A Snug Little Flock: The Social Origins of the Riel Resistance of 1869–1870.* Winnipeg: Watson and Dwyer, 1991.

Renfree, Harry. *Heritage and Horizon: The Baptist Story in Canada*. Mississauga: Canadian Baptist Federation, 1988.

Robertson, James Tyler. "'A Very Present Help in Trouble': The Ontario Baptists and the Fenian Invasion, 1866." In *Baptists and Public Life*, edited by Gordon L. Heath and Michael Haykin. Eugene OR: Pickwick Press, forthcoming.

Semple, Neil. *The Lord's Dominion: The History of Canadian Methodism*. Montreal/Kingston: McGill-Queen's University Press, 1996.

Sprague, Douglas. "The Manitoba Land Question, 1870–1882," in Bowsfield, (ed.), *Riel*, 62–77.

Stacey, C. P. *Canada and the Age of Conflict.* Vol. 1, *1867–1921*. Toronto: University of Toronto Press, 1984.

The Story of Louis Riel: The Rebel Chief. Toronto: J. S. Robertson and Brothers, 1885.

[*MJTM* 10 (2008–2009) R1–R3]

BOOK REVIEW

Michael P. Knowles. *We Preach Not Ourselves: Paul on Proclamation*. Grand Rapids, MI: Brazos Press, 2008. 256 pp. Pbk. US$24.99.

In *We Preach Not Ourselves: Paul on Proclamation*, Michael Knowles distills a spirituality of preaching from the apostle Paul's imitation of Christ as portrayed in 2 Cor 1:1—6:13. The preacher's stance modeled by Paul is Christocentric and cruciform. The preacher is constantly humbled (humiliated in the best sense of the word) at the foot of the cross, dying to self (to self-importance and self-reliance), resting solely upon Christ and the resurrecting power of the Holy Spirit. This is not an easy read for preachers. It is a reminder of both the gravity of the task and the continual need for self-emptying that allows God to fill the preacher with new life and power. If a preacher is ever effective, it is because God breathes life into the sermon.

Knowles delights with his careful exposition and commentary on Scripture, illuminating both Paul's language and the social context of the epistle. An example of the careful exegesis that graces the majority of the book and is its main strength can be found in Knowles's twelve-page treatment of 2 Cor 3:18 (pp. 122–38). In the subject "we all" he finds confirmation that cruciform preaching effects both preacher and congregation. The phrase "unveiled faces" allows Knowles to examine the tradition of Moses veiling himself upon coming down from Mt. Sinai. This tradition is contrasted with the new reality that in Christ the glory that was veiled with Moses (to hide its fading impermanence) has now been permanently unveiled. Knowles explains this allusion for modern-day readers who might otherwise lose the significance of the reference. He then comments helpfully on the biblical understanding of the "glory of the Lord." Paul says to the Corinthian church that "we behold this glory as in a mirror" and Knowles is able to expound the meaning and significance of the metaphor of glory reflected in a city well-known for its bronze products, which included mirrors. In the same manner, Knowles makes detailed commentary on the remaining phrases of v. 8: "transformed into the same image," "from glory to glory," and "as from the Lord, the Spirit." In each case, Knowles finds significant theological meaning and homiletical import in Paul's phrasing and choice of words.

With an eye towards preaching, Knowles examines Paul as a counterintuitive leader and model who, having experienced his own affliction, embraces suffering as invitation to and anticipation of God's grace. The preacher suffers as a direct response to God's initiative or call in his or her life. Knowles asks with Paul, "Who can preach?" Considering the cruciform model set out for the preacher one might equally ask, "Who would want to preach?" Only someone captured by Christ and overcome by the vocation will submit to the sacrifices that accompany the task, refusing to become a peddler of the word, refusing to preach a gospel that is comforting or aesthetically pleasing, preaching only Jesus Christ the crucified Lord.

The apostle is also the model for God using the unseemly to effect change in the world. Paul does not dispute his detractors in Corinth when they point out his flaws, rather he points all the more to the grace of a God who works through such an unimpressive vessel. Lifting up the cruciform Lord's example of power in weakness, the apostle holds together through faith numerous tensions: affliction and consolation, triumph and captivity, confidence and conviction, spirit and flesh, sacred and secular, heaven and earth, time and eternity, seen and unseen, and now and not yet. These tensions are not resolved as those outside of Christ would expect, but are held together in Christ in a manner that leads to glory and hope. Faith in Christ preserves the preacher within these tensions and transforms the congregation towards Christ-like glory. The preacher knows by experience the consolation of which he or she speaks. This personal knowledge verifies what is possible and made available through Jesus Christ, who is the initiator, the content and the sustainer of the proclamation. As with preaching, the community's movement to glory depends not upon its own actions but upon the actions of God. The wonder continues to be that Sunday by Sunday and week by week God continues to use preachers who make themselves available to God as vessels, making them God's ambassadors on earth.

Just as Paul responds to supposed super-apostles in Corinth, Knowles reacts to modern preachers and ministries that appear too glossy, successful, or prestigious. Knowles wants to lift up and encourage the regular mundane sacrifices of pastors of small congregations who will never get much notice or esteem. Preachers discouraged by the difficulties and sacrifices of their calling are reminded that these are normal, even to be expected, in faithful response to their calling, and preachers are encouraged and strengthened by a spirituality that is rooted in Christ and contemplates the cross. Knowles would seem to suggest that congregations and denominations concerned about preaching should emphasize spiritual development, particularly Christ-centered cruciform discipleship, at least as much if not more than oratory, rhetoric, or communication skills.

Those sharing Knowles's biblical assumptions and worldview will find support in this book for the reliance upon God necessary for the task of preaching. Knowles offers an interesting heuristic device in his examination of 2 Corinthians to discern the apostle's homiletical method behind the text. This is a worthy contribution to the larger task of lifting out biblical examples of preachers and homiletical method. *We Preach Not Ourselves*, well-grounded in Scripture, looks up from the text regularly to comment on the current state of preaching, the voice of a New Testament scholar offered to anyone interested and concerned about faithful and effective preaching.

Steven Schumm
Pastor, Hamilton Mennonite Church

[*MJTM* 10 (2008–2009) R4–R6]

Book Review

Ronald J. Sider. *I Am Not a Social Activist: Making Jesus the Agenda.* Waterloo, ON: Herald Press, 2008. 211 pp. Pbk. CDN$16.99.

There is today, within the church and the broader culture, a movement toward greater concern for issues of poverty and social justice. This is seen in mass movements like the "Make Poverty History" campaign, the church sponsored "Micah Challenge" and the social consciousness of celebrities like U2's Bono, and actress Angelina Jolie. While the emergence of this renewed social consciousness is refreshing, Ron Sider has been a dedicated social activist with a passion for justice since the late 1960's. What further distinguishes Sider is that, as an evangelical Christian, he was far ahead of his time as an advocate on social issues. His book *I Am Not a Social Activist* addresses what may be *the* crucial question for our current evangelical milieu: how do evangelicals approach the issue of social activism in a theologically responsible and constructive way?

The book is a selected collection of columns that Sider wrote between 1993 and 2007 for *Prism* magazine, a publication of the organization Evangelicals for Social Action. Sider founded this organization and continues to serve with it as a committed voice for the marginalized and as a mobilizer for evangelicals to get engaged with social issues. This slim volume covers a number of topics germane to that mission, including spirituality, Christology, a theology of social action, and the place of evangelism in social justice ministry.

Sider is clear about where his ultimate allegiance stands when he explains the title by stating, "I am not a social activist, I am a disciple of Jesus Christ" (p. 21). Sider goes on to emphasize his belief that a Christ-centered faith coupled with evangelistic passion is central to any appropriate approach to Christian social action. This challenges perceptions that social action is the realm of liberal or mainline churches and not a priority for evangelicals. Sider has always been a firmly committed evangelical and in the first section of the book he makes a clear plea for a Jesus-centered spirituality that will underpin the dual responsibilities of evangelism and care for the needy, both of which are part of what the church is called to do.

The book is a combination of philosophical reflection on the foundations of Christian social action and practical advice on how churches and individuals can become more involved in justice issues. One chapter, entitled "Eight Keys to Holistic Ministry," offers highly applicable insights on how a holistic ministry can be constructed. Other chapters reflect Sider's desire to see evangelicals develop a philosophy of social action. He also has a section on politics and offers some views on how Christians can (and should) engage in the political process.

Sider writes with a winsome and gracious style, however some of the book includes edgier sections that give a scathing critique of contemporary evangelicalism. In his chapter, "Are Evangelical Leaders on the Way to Hell?" Sider wonders if today's evangelical leaders come anywhere near spending the same amount of time as Jesus did on preaching about concern for the poor and needy. Later in the book he expresses his opinion that mainstream evangelicalism is "largely conformed to the world" (p. 119) in its lack of concern for the poor, the environment, and gender and racial equality. This combination of philosophical rumination, practical insight, and prophetic questioning give the book a highly readable, thought-provoking quality.

Perhaps what commends the book most is the fact that Sider captures a growing spirit within contemporary evangelicalism toward social justice. As a long-time practitioner, Sider speaks not as someone who is just caught up in an emerging trend, but as one who was there long before most of us came around. Thus, his musings, captured in this current volume, are the voice of experience reflecting on years in the trenches and offering guiding thoughts to those who want to join the mission. He is an elder statesman in what is becoming a broader evangelical movement that is no longer just concerned about one or two key social issues (often abortion and gay rights), but also wants to address issues of poverty, equality, and the care of creation.

If there is a weakness to the book, it is one that Sider himself confesses. He writes in the preface that a collection of essays such as the one he is offering is by nature limited in its ability to develop an argument, respond to alternate viewpoints, and suggest in-depth strategies for application of the author's ideas. Indeed, while this book is a good introduction to Sider's thought, and a helpful primer for thinking about Christian social engagement, it lacks the kind of in-depth analysis and careful argument that elevates a book to something beyond simply good reading. *I Am Not a Social Activist* offers many interesting thoughts and some compelling challenges; however, it is not a systematic consideration of the emerging social action movement within evangelical Christianity or a blueprint for ongoing development of that movement. It is offered as a compilation of thoughts from one of the movement's veteran leaders, and as such it has its place as a helpful contribution to the conversation.

Something further to be aware of is the highly American nature of the book. While Sider is a Canadian by birth, his work and life have been located in the U.S. and he writes from that perspective. This is not bad, however readers from other countries will note that some of the cultural and political norms discussed in the book may be far different in their context.

The rediscovery of a social conscience is an encouraging development in evangelicalism today. Ron Sider is one of those clear-minded, balanced evangelicals who combines evangelistic passion and social concern with theological reflection and pastoral pragmatism. This adds up to a voice worth listening to, and *I Am Not a Social Activist*, as an introduction to Sider's work, may leave you wanting to pursue the issues further by reading another of Sider's more detailed volumes.

Lee Beach
McMaster Divinity College

[*MJTM* 10 (2008–2009) R7–R8]

Book Review

Don E. Saliers. *Music and Theology*. Nashville, TN: Abingdon Press, 2007. xii + 83 pp. Pbk. US$10.50.

The powerful relationship of music and the sacred has long been recognized. The Old Testament illustrates music's ability to enhance the praise of God (e.g., Ps 150); Paul recommended singing psalms, hymns, and spiritual songs (Col 3:16); and Martin Luther wrote, "next to the word of God, music deserves the highest praise" (*Liturgy and Hymns*, Luther's Works 53:323). Liturgical texts set to music are imbued with greater emotive and associational power than when they are merely spoken. But this age-old acknowledgement of music's profound role in religious experience has yielded surprisingly few accessible writings on the subject. For the most part, studies in religious music have been written by scholars for scholars, leaving general readers without a concise introduction to the theories of the field. And while it can be argued that sacred music is more apt for experience than discussion, there is much to be gained from a better understanding of this essential aid to prayer and praise.

Fortunately, Don E. Saliers, a senior scholar of theology and worship at Candler School of Theology, has written a brief and engaging primer addressing the major issues in worship, theology, and music. As an overview of scholarship and an introduction to his own thought, this book is everything it should be: readable yet substantive, concise yet comprehensive, broad yet detailed. The book's seven chapters address wide-ranging topics, including music and the body, the intersection of theology and songs of social justice, and the often-blurry line between what are typically called "sacred" and "secular" musical styles.

Saliers investigates a number of traditional and popular musical sources—from Bach to John Coltrane—building a case that theology requires music. He notes that while the theologian's realm is language, the subject of theology is beyond words. Music, however, expresses the verbally inexpressible, helping to clarify spiritual truths that may seem overly complex or even far-fetched. As Sailers writes, "[we] are asked to say some things that we don't truly think we believe until we sing them, or hear them in appropriately complex activities" (p. 6). Elsewhere he explains that when "great theologians wish to speak of the deepest realities, they move toward poetry and music—heightened speech—as an attempt to 'sound' spiritual matters" (p. 72). But he also cautions that not all music inspires contemplation, functions theologically, or is appropriate for religious reflection. Musical settings of liturgy in particular must be true to the message and spirit of the words.

Of special interest is Saliers's lucid discussion of hymns (ch. 4). Sacred songs are often characterized by simplicity and redundancy, qualities that make them ideal for religious messages. Especially in Christian hymn traditions, pithy verses convey theological viewpoints argued elsewhere, or emphasize religious themes such as praise, commitment, longing, and lament. By the careful partnership of music and words, an effective song can capture succinctly the essence of both religious ideas and the sacred moment, producing what Saliers calls a "theological miniature" (p. 36). And because hymns are hedged by the demands of unity and clarity, they serve an important didactic role.

The greatest strength of this book is that it is succinct without being superficial. However, the book's brevity led the publisher not to include an index, which would have enhanced the text. A list of suggested readings would also have been valuable, especially given Saliers's four decades as a teacher of theology and worship. Still, these would just be added bonuses for a book that is, in both content and style, perhaps the most useful general text on music and theology to date. Its intended readership is wide, from undergraduate and seminary students to interested laypeople, clergy, and church musicians, and its value is immense.

Jonathan L. Friedmann,
Academy for Jewish Religion, Los Angeles, California

[*MJTM* 10 (2008–2009) R9–R12]

BOOK REVIEW

Craig L. Blomberg and Mariam J. Kamell. *James*. Zondervan Exegetical Commentary on the New Testament. Grand Rapids: Zondervan, 2008. 280 pp. Hdbk. US$24.99.

James by Craig L. Blomberg and Mariam J. Kamell offers a useful scholarly resource to teachers and pastors. The emphasis of the commentary is on applying James's teaching on wealth and poverty to contemporary church life. The themes of trial and temptation along with wisdom and speech are also noted by the authors. The simple layout of the text helps mark out primary and supportive material in the epistle. The contemporary applications are helpful, if at times overdone. Ultimately, the commentary delivers on scholarly competence and relevant application, but the brevity of the work necessitates abbreviation of several discussions along the way.

The series layout organizes the text into a logical schematic. This diagram helps to show cause, conditions, manner, and temporal/spatial description among other things. Furthermore, it places the clauses into a logical framework, making apparent which are the supporting and main clauses. The diagram could be useful for sermon and lesson preparation, in that it illustrates main points for emphasis. Also, the diagram is a good refresher for the role of various grammatical features of the Greek text. It shows the implications of conjunction choice, clause structure, and qualification. The main participants in the sentence (subject, predicate, complement) are placed in bold. The diagram of the text provides a means of thinking about the sentence structure and logical relations of clauses.

Unfortunately, the logical schematic is unable to show several discourse and stylistic features of the text. The diagram does not make the prominent use of hook words evident ("hook words" repeat the ending term of a sentence at the beginning of the next sentence) and only some of the hook words used in James are identified in the verse-by-verse comment. This stylistic feature of James is a key stylistic element of the epistle. Likewise features such as word order are hard to represent on the outline. While the semantic implications of Greek word order are still somewhat under debate, diagrams that move pastors and scholars away from the actual word order of the text do not help. These diagrams do, however, provide logical relations that are based on the sentence grammar.

Blomberg and Kamell are able to distill three key themes from the text of James. In contrast to Martin Dibelius's form-critical treatment, the move toward seeing the unity of the epistle is refreshing. The structure of the epistle, based on the assertion of unity, is both plausible in an academic sense and useful in a pastoral sense. Blomberg and Kamell suggest that wealth and poverty, wisdom and speech, and trials and temptations compose the most prominent themes for the epistle. In terms of explaining the text, these issues consistently recur throughout. Furthermore, almost all of what occurs in the epistle can be viewed in terms of these themes. This illustrates the compositional unity of the epistle. As far as application is concerned, these issues not only explain the historical document, but reflect key issues in living the Christian life.

The theme of wealth and poverty is emphasized by Blomberg and Kamell. They argue for its prominence by suggesting an arching chiastic structure that places this topic at the middle of the discourse. Also, several of the other themes contain elements of poverty and wealth in their discussions. This issue remains a perennial topic in Western Christianity and James's valuable perspective is skillfully applied in many ways.

Blomberg and Kamell attempt, somewhat awkwardly, to unify the three themes in the epistle. While the commentary clearly emphasizes wealth and poverty, the final attempt to create a unifying principle for the three themes centers around the doctrine of God, specifically that God is unswerving in his judgment and mercy. As such, Christianity should hold to this same unswerving demeanor. First, the authors do not address the issue of unity in terms of the three major themes asserted, leaving the reader to question the value of the categories proposed for understanding. Furthermore, the commentary asserts that God is both giver of mercy and gifts and judge/lawgiver in James. It is odd that the key unifying principle, then, is the unity of God's purpose. Finally, a more traditional unifying principle is that of Christian maturity and completeness. While this completeness is rooted in the attribute of God, it encompasses a doctrinal and ethical program for the Christian community.

Blomberg and Kamell do not always note important dissenting opinions. The series is designed to be a resource for the church leader as well as the scholar and as such has carefully maintained a style and level of discussion commensurate with this purpose. Unfortunately, this means that several more in-depth discussions were not presented in the work. For instance, Blomberg and Kamell side with Davids's structure with three unifying themes. However, Luke Timothy Johnson argues for a singularity to the structure of the epistle. In contrast, Dibelius's form-critical approach sees the text as a redaction of several disparate units. Blomberg and Kamell spare the reader much of this discussion, a decision that has significant implications for how one understands the statements of the epistle.

Application of the text is a paramount concern for the authors. Blomberg and Kamell see in James's epistle a call to work against systemic inequality. This involves both an emphasis on Christian benevolence and a reining in of the drive to acquire wealth. Furthermore, they advocate a political perspective that must necessarily reject libertarianism in favor of a liberation theology perspective, albeit qualified. Most prominently they encourage suburban churches to involve themselves with urban issues.

The applications of the text are sometimes trite. For example, the authors' casual mention of the "rape" of the environment makes implications unsupported by James's text. Furthermore, this clichéd idiom does not provide the effect that a longer explication of the issue and its relation to James could provide. Also, the attempt to move from personal to systemic ethics is a bit clumsy. For example, Blomberg and Kamell use the illustration of food waste from restaurants to show the excess of Western culture. The comparison of restaurant patrons to the wealthy landowner who withholds wages from the destitute is a bit of a stretch, especially when more apt illustrations are available. Many of the applications are very pertinent to the Christian situation, but an overvaluation of models based on systemic ethics makes some of the applications unwieldy for the church leader.

Blomberg and Kamell admirably negotiate the liberation readings of James from an evangelical perspective. This commentary addresses key ethical issues raised by the epistle, including their placement in Arminian and Calvinist traditions. However, many will find the ethical aspect of the commentary merely a starting point for further discussion and inquiry. A competent, yet brief, treatment of the themes of "wisdom and speech," and "trials and temptations," is included. While Blomberg and Kamell state that wealth and poverty is the most prominent theme, their attempt to elucidate a singular theme does not take this into account. Useful applications of many of the texts are explicated, but some of the applications are extreme. Theme and logic drive the commentary as opposed to style and discourse. The brevity of the commentary has benefits and drawbacks.

Overall, this commentary is a useful resource for the pastor who wants a scholarly opinion, but does not want to get bogged down in issues of history, phrasing, and structure.

Brad Williams
McMaster Divinity College

[*MJTM* 10 (2008–2009) R13–R15]

Book Review

Gary M. Burge, Lynn H. Cohick, and Gene L. Green. *The New Testament in Antiquity*. Grand Rapids: Zondervan, 2009. 479 pp. Hdbk. US$49.99; CDN $53.99.

This impressive New Testament introduction and survey was written by three professors from Wheaton College, designed as a textbook for North American undergraduate students. As would be expected from the background of the authors, the book seeks to stand firmly within the tradition of evangelical biblical interpretation.

The book's student-friendly features include: almost 500 full-color maps, photos, charts, and drawings relevant to the subject matter; numerous sidebars; chapters short enough to be read through in 30 to 60 minutes; minimal footnotes; discussion questions and a short, graded bibliography at the end of each chapter; and a heavy book construction that guarantees long usefulness of the volume whether it is kept for reference or passed on to succeeding classes of students. The book's 27 chapters divide the material into units that can be covered, two a week, in a typical semester. There are special chapters on the historical reliability of the story of Jesus (including a sidebar on the Jesus Seminar), the life of Paul (with a sidebar on the New Perspective on Paul), and the textual history of the New Testament. Other important issues in New Testament study today are also explained to orient students who are in the early stages of familiarity with this field of study. Scripture and subject indexes make it easy for readers to find material they need.

The book has some special features that mark it off from similar introductions. Most books start the discussion of each book of the New Testament with matters like author and date. *The New Testament in Antiquity* begins with the message of the book, and saves these matters for the end of each chapter. This is a clear indication that the authors see the message of the New Testament as being more central and important, while author and date considerations are more peripheral. This goes along with their insistence that students also read the entire New Testament text along with the textbook.

Another feature, reflected in the title, is the book's sustained interest in the context of the New Testament in the ancient Mediterranean world. There are separate chapters or sections on methodology, the historical background, geography, the Jewish cultural environment, and Greco-Roman culture. The wealth of excellent illustrations support this emphasis. The authors have drawn heavily on the work of the Context Group, a group of scholars dedicated to using the insights of social science to understand biblical events and relationships. References to an "honor and shame" culture and "patronage," for example, are common. The book emphasizes that reading the New Testament is a cross-cultural exercise, in which we cannot always assume that we understand what is going on just from our own background.

A third feature is the use of illustrations of ancient coins. One of the authors has expertise in coins, and they are pictured often, especially in their capacity as vehicles of propaganda. The theme logo of the book is the Roman coin depicting *Judea capta*.

The main criticisms of this book, understandably, are due to its attempt to cover so much and keep it so simple. Nuances that many would think are important have been omitted. To keep the book to the desired length, much that some teachers and scholars would like to see in an introduction has been left out. A brief survey of internet reviewers reveals one unhappy that the treatment of rhetoric is weak, another thinks there should be more on hermeneutics, while a third wanted more on women. At least this leaves room for a teacher to demonstrate his or her worth to the students by adding material not in the book!

On the down side, I think the book is sometimes over-enthusiastic in its embrace of social-science criticism. For example, it is true that the patronage system operated in Roman society, but to uncritically accept that it operated in Jewish circles to the extent that the relationship of Jesus to God the Father can be understood in terms of patronage (p. 170) is certainly stretching the evidence. As the field of social-science criticism continues to evolve, some of the ways the book treats this approach may become outdated.

The labels of some of the illustrations are also misleading. Here are a few examples. Apart from the embarrassing identification of POxy 52 as P52 on page 16 (an error that the editors are aware of and have promised to amend in future printings), the caption on a photograph of a manuscript page of the Gospel of Thomas on page 112 says that it was discovered in 1945 at Oxyrhynchus. Actually, some Greek fragments of the Gospel of Thomas were discovered at Oxyrhynchus in 1897, 1903, and 1905, whereas the Coptic document pictured was found at Nag Hammadi in 1945. On page 377, the caption for the picture from Pompeii of Terentius Neo says that the woman holds a book, whereas actually she has a wax tablet in her hand. On page 451 is a photograph of the sheet of a Greek harmony of the Gospels found at Dura Europos. The caption says it is a sheet of Tatian's Diatessaron, found in 1935, whereas the actual date of discovery was 1933. Neither is there any hint of the controversy over whether this is actually part of Tatian's work.

These errors are probably due to the authors' and editors' lack of specialized expertise in areas somewhat peripheral to the thrust of the book. The book is still a fine introductory text, but due to such minor errors has less value as a reference volume. Perhaps future editions of the book will be able to rectify this, as users who do have the expertise point out the errors. Most North American evangelical teachers and students of New Testament Introduction and Survey will enjoy using this book. It is so contextualized for America, however, that it might need adaptation to be completely suitable for classrooms in other parts of the world.

Lois Dow
McMaster Divinity College

[*MJTM* 10 (2008–2009) R16–R19]

Book Review

Elaine A. Heath. *The Mystic Way of Evangelism: A Contemplative Vision for Christian Outreach.* Grand Rapids: Baker Academic, 2008. 207 pp. Pbk. US$19.99.

Heath, who is McCreless Assistant Professor of Evangelism and Director of the Center for the Advanced Study and Practice of Evangelism at Perkins School of Theology, Southern Methodist University (in Dallas, Texas), typifies the post-modern allergy to "programmatic evangelism"—familiar to many evangelicals—that (at best) promises numerical and spiritual success in response to a specified methodology or (at worst) trades on specious promises of blessing and overt threats of hell. In conscious contrast to such approaches, Heath roots her own proposals in a proper appreciation of orthodox Christian spirituality (which she prefers to call "mysticism") that has as its twin goals inward transformation and outward action in the form of compassionate mission or evangelism.

Her study is divided into three sections: "Purgation," "Illumination," and "Union." The first of these, consisting of a single chapter, proposes that "A dark night of the soul is descending on the church in the United States" (p. 25). By this Heath means that the American (mainline? Protestant? Evangelical?) church has fallen into numerical and financial decline, spiritual torpor, and moral irrelevance in relation to its cultural context. More specifically, she proposes that such decline is in fact divinely initiated, intended to foster impatience with formulaic religion and inspire a deeper yearning for a more direct and authentic encounter with God.

Each chapter of the second section, "Illumination," draws on the insights of a pair of mystics or theologians. So, for instance, "Love is God's Meaning" derives from Julian of Norwich a "therapeutic view of redemption" (that original sin derives from prior woundedness, so that redemption entails healing rather than condemnation) and from Hans Urs von Balthasar a non-punitive model of the atonement that hopes for the salvation of all humanity. On this basis Heath offers a narrative reading of Genesis 3 that likens the Fall of Adam and Eve to an experience of sexual abuse (whereby misplaced trust leads to profound wounding, and wounding in turn to dysfunctional coping strategies). One limitation of this illustration, however, is that it explores the nature of the human predicament without further clarifying the implications of a non-punitive or therapeutic vision of redemption.

Chapter 3, "Broken Bread and Poured Out Wine," appeals to Phoebe Palmer, the nineteenth-century Methodist reformer, and a Russian Orthodox priest by the name of Father Arseny, who was imprisoned for twenty years under Stalin. Both of these model absolute consecration to God amidst deep suffering, which Heath sees as the basis for a kind of evangelism that is rooted in the example of personal holiness.

Next are two twentieth-century mystics, the Quaker Thomas R. Kelly and Henri Nouwen, the Dutch Roman Catholic priest known both for his writing and for his membership in the L'Arche Daybreak community in Toronto. Both suffered from persistent insecurity, anxiety, and depression, and both found solace via prayer and contemplation in profound experiences of God's love. Just so, Heath contends, North American Christians need to discover their true identity by "soaking in the infinite love of God" (p. 82).

Chapter 5, "Healing the Threefold Wound," relates the painful history of a nineteenth-century African-American evangelist, Julia Foote, as an antidote to what Heath sees as the persistent "patriarchy, racism, and classism"—the "threefold wound"—of North American Protestantism (p. 90). From a much earlier era, Mechthild of Magdeburg (who shares with Foote many visionary experiences) also claimed a powerful a ministry that others in her day believed should be the sole preserve of men. Rather than directly addressing the church's mission, this discussion provides a call to corporate ecclesiastical repentance.

In the final chapter from this section, "Redeeming the Earth," "St. Bonaventure and John Woolman offer a vision of redemption in which environmental ethics and salvation go hand in hand" (p. 102). Added to their examples is that of David Saw Wah, a Burmese refugee who—albeit in non-religious terms—demonstrates a kind of "eco-evangelism" that liberates creation from exploitation.

Heath's vision is wide-ranging and, for that reason, necessarily imprecise. She offers illustrations in place of instructions, an inspiring vision of what the love of God makes possible rather than concrete details or specific directions. This will no doubt prove confusing to some readers, even as others will chafe at the generalized appropriation of insights from practitioners far removed from the needs and circumstances of present-day Western Protestantism.

Part Three, "Union," offers some initial responses to such concerns. Heath is inspired particularly by a small community of the Sisters of Charity in Dallas, whose primary ministry is to pray for the residents of their local community and to serve them with the compassion of Christ. She advocates selflessness and self-emptying (*kenosis*), suggesting the appropriateness of bi-vocational ministry, the radical down-sizing of congregational ministry, and an emphasis on service and community formation more than the Sunday worship service (p. 137). Much of this is conveyed via the imaginative narrative of "Sam," a thrice-divorced newcomer who finds an unexpected welcome at "First Church."

While there is little to disagree with in her treatment, I found myself wishing that Heath had followed her convictions considerably further. As indicated, her practical suggestions revolve (ecclesiastically) around flexibility in congregational leadership structures and (missiologically) around the need for compassion in our relationships with one another. What seemed missing, however, was a sufficient engagement with the kind of vibrant, passionate, and all-consuming mysticism that is necessary to sustain this counter-cultural vision of church and ministry. In particular, links to the ten mystics and practical theologians described in the previous section seemed rather tenuous.

To be fair, Heath briefly explores aspects of *lectio divina* and contemplative prayer, calling for a "new Pentecostalism [that] would mean radical changes in how the church understands gender, race, and social location" (p. 160). Such a movement, she proposes, "would mean an egalitarian approach to leadership in the church, a preference for new church starts in disadvantaged urban and rural settings, and significant emphasis on ministries that prevent and heal the violence of the threefold wound" (p. 161). Likewise she offers concrete proposals for the practice of eco-evangelism, rooted in a theology of creational stewardship.

But the danger in such discussion is that it risks—unintentionally to be sure—becoming simply another strategy or method, rather than a radical and holistic orientation to the life of Jesus, which is the true focus and source of Christian mysticism. The "Union" to which the title of this final section refers is, after all, first and foremost mystical union with Christ. To say this does not diminish the value either of this study or of Heath's larger vision, but simply acknowledges that North Americans in particular seem culturally prone to a kind of reductionistic pragmatism, especially so when it comes to matters of church renewal. Accordingly, readers might wish to study *The Mystic Way of Evangelism* hand-in-hand with original works by some of the writers that Heath cites, other classic resources for spiritual discipline and renewal, or (given the intended audience of this book) the works of contemporary Protestant authors such as Henry Blackaby, Richard Foster, or Dallas Willard.

Michael P. Knowles
McMaster Divinity College

[*MJTM* 10 (2008–2009) R20–R23]

Book Review

Keith Ward. *God and the Philosophers*. Minneapolis: Fortress Press, 2009. 153 pp. Pbk. US$20.00; CDN$24.63.

Amid the vitriolic verbiage of certain atheistic philosophers and biologists, one can easily come away with the perception that Western philosophy, both modern and traditional, has been predominantly hostile toward theistic belief. It is with the hope of clearing up such misunderstandings that Keith Ward has penned the slim volume *God and the Philosophers*, an adaptation of his 2008 Sarum Lectures. In it, he aims to defend a singular thesis, namely, that the general consensus of the Western philosophical tradition accepts what he calls "the God conclusion," which posits that there is a perfect spiritual reality that gave rise to, and now continues to sustain, the natural world. This he sets out to do by chronologically examining the thought of a number of key thinkers from Plato to Schopenhauer, along the way drawing attention to their (more or less) theistic presuppositions and straightening out common misreadings.

The back cover notes that the material has been adapted "for a wide readership," and this claim appears to be substantiated. For instance, terms that would be common knowledge for the undergraduate philosophy major—e.g., idealism, critical realism, and materialism—are almost always introduced with concise definitions. Moreover, Ward's tone is consistently genial and anecdotal, even humorous at times. As a result, it is likely that those with a Bachelor's degree in the humanities will have few problems understanding the bulk of the material. The confessional stance of the book's intended "wide readership" is slightly more difficult to discern, although as it is a publication of Fortress Press—the official publishing house of the Evangelical Lutheran Church in America—those in ministry and those in the church looking to deepen their roots in religious philosophy are likely targets. Non-believers in search of an account that runs counter to the "common" wisdom cannot be ruled out either.

One concern that surfaces even after a brief perusal of the book is that the material can meander at times. On the one hand, Ward is attempting to make the thinkers he is presenting accessible, so he begins most chapters with a brief background; on the other, he is looking to uphold his thesis by showing the pervasiveness of the God conclusion in Western philosophy, and thus quickly moves well beyond the rudiments. To add to the copious digressions intrinsic to this approach, he aims to defend many "lost causes" (such as the possibility that Plato was a proto-libertarian of sorts) along the way. Nevertheless, perhaps pressing the book for a rigid formalism misconstrues Ward's intentions, for excursions aside, Ward is by and large successful at justifying his thesis. Salient among the book's eleven chapters in this regard are the ninth and tenth. In the ninth, Ward demonstrates how the first "German atheist," Arthur Schopenhauer, actually held to the idea of a comprehensive spiritual reality that was more a rejection of the popular, anthropomorphic misconception of God than of the idea of God himself; consequently, room is left even in his framework for a more nuanced construal of God. In chapter 10 Ward sets forth the contradictions in Nietzsche, and goes on to show negatively what ultimately happens when the God conclusion is rejected—the imperilment of reason, the loss of dignity to the human person, and so on. By cutting off the flow "upstream," Ward is accordingly able to undermine the position of later atheists, and hence to present the God conclusion in a more attractive light. Positive contributions to the thesis from Plato, Aquinas, Descartes, and even Kant further strengthen Ward's case.

A central theme, one correlated to Ward's thesis, is the philosophical theory broadly identified as "idealism." Beginning with Plato and his concept of the Ideas or Forms, Ward traces the way in which this theory has, in one shape or another, remained part of the Western philosophical tradition, being a keystone in the systems of thinkers as diverse as Plato, Descartes, Berkeley, Kant, Hegel, and even Schopenhauer. Idealism contains as a posit that mind or consciousness is somehow fundamental to all reality. Without finite, human minds to process the material world, "this world of more or less solid coloured and extended objects in motion dissolves into a sea of probability-waves in a multi-dimensional logical space" (p. 48). But one can take this concept even further, as Western philosophers often have. That the world as we experience it is not "an accidental concatenation of chance occurrences" (p. 46)—that material reality is even intelligible at all—suggests that as we explore the natural world we are actually inquiring into a supreme cosmic mind, the very mind of God. Faith, then, tends in the direction of upholding the power of human reason, where the ideas of atheistic thinkers like Hume—*contra* the misconceptions bandied about by iconoclastic secular humanists today—actually detract from it. By bringing idealism into the discussion, Ward is able to show that even when Western philosophers have spoken on topics other than God, their treatment of these topics has consistently presupposed, indeed, positively demanded, the God conclusion.

A particular strength is the way in which Ward makes the writings of the philosophical "greats" of the Western tradition not only accessible, but palatable for further intellectual expeditions. Of Hegel, for instance, Ward concedes that his writing "is excessively complex and obscure," and yet he goes on to deftly demonstrate how "its main ideas are actually rather simple" (p. 90). The same rings true for each thinker introduced. That is by no means to say that this book is a walk in the park, but in every instance Ward provides the reader with the tools necessary to get a handle on the material being presented. Thus, even if the primary purpose of the book is to uphold the God conclusion, it nevertheless succeeds in the concomitant aim of serving as an accessible primer on some of the towering figures in Western philosophy.

It should be clear by now, though, that this book is almost only incidentally related to Christianity. While the Christian faith is an irreducible aspect of the Western philosophical tradition, the erasure of the sparse biblical quotes and Christian-God references that dot the book would make it equally applicable to other monotheistic traditions. Indeed, the book is every bit one of philosophy, with little relation to the seminary discipline of Christian theology—for better or for worse.

And that leads to a significant criticism: the careful reader will note that the "God" to which Ward seems to lend support diverges at times from the "God of the Bible" and the God of the Christian theological tradition. For instance, in dealing with the question of evil and suffering, Ward suggests that there might "be something in the divine nature that necessitates the creation of a universe of free agents" (p. 71). He goes even further, however, positing that God might not even be "free to create a universe without evil in it" (p. 71). Such ideas stand in clear contradiction to the traditional exposition of the doctrine of Creation, in which God creates sovereignly and with no obligation on his own part. A little later, in treating Hegel's thought, Ward approvingly writes, "it may be necessary for Spirit to originate [the] world, if it is to realise more completely its own possible perfections" (p. 99). Clearly, the gist of these remarks impugns traditional Christian views concerning the total sovereignty of God. If God's own being inherently contains need, that is, imperfection, what basis do we have for believing that he will be able to set to rights this cosmos, so replete with seemingly insuperable evil and suffering? At any rate, Ward excuses himself: "philosophers have something of a reputation for independence of mind and scepticism, and they usually dislike being thought of as defenders of any sort of orthodoxy" (p. 2). Apparently he views himself as no exception.

All told, however, there is much to be commended about this book. As an accessible introduction to Western philosophy, it provides the amateur enthusiast with a wading pool in which to get the feet wet. And as a demonstration of the consentient God conclusion in the Western tradition, the book succeeds admirably on both academic and popular levels. Ministers and lay leaders alike would do well in purchasing it, if only as a starting point for further study in a discipline that has time and again been the "handmaid," not the chief antagonist, of Christian theology.

Robert J. Hong
Wycliffe College